COTTAGE TALES

Also by John Clare

The Midsummer Cushion
edited by Kelsey Thornton & Anne Tibble

JOHN CLARE
Cottage Tales

Edited by Eric Robinson, David Powell and P.M.S. Dawson

The Mid Northumberland Arts Group
Carcanet Press
1993

This edition first published in 1993 by
Mid Northumberland Arts Group, Wansbeck Square,
Ashington, Northumberland NE63 9XL
and Carcanet Press Limited,
208-212 Corn Exchange Buildings,
Manchester M4 3BQ.

ISBN 0 904790 78 9 (MidNAG)
ISBN 1 85754 032 8 (Carcanet)
A CIP catalogue record for this book
is available from the British Library.

The publishers acknowledge financial assistance from
Northern Arts and the Arts Council of Great Britain.

Set in 10pt Palatino by Bryan Williamson, Frome, Somerset
Printed and bound in England by SRP Ltd, Exeter

Contents

Acknowledgements

The text of this book was prepared with the help of a grant from the National Endowment for the Humanities (Editions), USA.

We wish to thank for their generous assistance the staff of the Peterborough Museum and Art Gallery, Northampton Central Public Library, the Pierpont Morgan Museum Library, the Berg Collection (New York Public Library) and several other libraries in Britain and the USA. Eric Robinson wishes to thank the University of Massachusetts at Boston for sabbatical leave. He also wishes to express his gratitude to George and Mary Dixon, Stanley Smith and Daphne and Godfrey Faux for their generous hospitality while he has been in England.

All of us wish to thank the John Clare Society for encouragement. (The secretary is Mary Moyse, The Stables, 1A West Street, Helpston, Peterborough, Cambridgeshire, PE6 7DU.) Finally we would like to express our gratitude to such booksellers as The Penguin Bookshop, Cathedral Square, Peterborough who faithfully stock a complete range of John Clare's writings.

Note on the Text

We have followed our usual practice of not tidying up Clare's poetry. We have left spelling, punctuation, grammar and vocabulary as he presented them, in the belief that the reader will quickly accustom herself/himself to them. Reading the verse aloud will usually make clear what Clare intended. Instead of 'he'd, she'd, he'll, she'll, I'm' etc., Clare usually wrote 'hed, shed, hell, shell, Im'. He also commonly left out the 'e' in words such as 'cared, scared, famed, shamed' to produce 'card, scard, famd, shamd', but the context will always make clear that he meant 'scared' and not 'scarred', or 'shamed' instead of 'shammed'. It was a characteristic of Clare's dialect to use the singular form of a noun sometimes for the plural: e.g. 'beast', where we would normally write 'beasts', so the reader needs to be alert to this. Where we think that a word or phrase needs to be explained we have done so in a glossary at the back of the book. If Clare intends a word such as 'shamed' to be a double syllable 'shamèd', he will write 'shamed' instead of 'shamd', but the fact that he includes the 'e' in such a word as 'cared' instead of writing 'card', does not necessarily mean that he intends a double syllable. The reader's ear should suffice. The lack of punctuation and the occasionally odd word-orders should not create much difficulty if the reader will read the verse aloud. Clare often omits capital letters and, infrequently, will use a capital letter at the beginning of a noun where we would not. He uses ampersands instead of the word 'and' or 'And', and we have preserved them.

In this edition, intended for the student and the general reader, we have not provided variants. They will be found in our Oxford English Text volumes, together with a full editorial apparatus and fuller annotation.

Introduction

Clare's narrative poems have not received much attention from his critics. The most extensive recent study of his work, by Tim Chilcott, does not mention them at all.[1] Mark Storey devotes no more than four pages to them, concluding with the telling remark that 'he doesn't seem to me to achieve anything like the moral weight of Crabbe'.[2] The same reference is made by Ian Jack, who claims that 'Like "The Cross Roads" in *The Village Minstrel*, the four tales in *The Shepherd's Calendar* owe a good deal to Crabbe'.[3] Clare was aware that he was likely to be accused of imitating Crabbe (mainly because of his use of the pentameter couplet), as he had been accused of imitating others: 'but let them say on for I despise them & their imitations'. He had certainly read Crabbe but had no wish to be confused with 'the parson poet': 'whats he know of the distresses of the poor musing over a snug coal fire in his parsonage box', he sneered.[4] As Karl Kroeber observes, 'Crabbe's portrait of rural existence is an external and rational one. He describes poor laborers and outcasts as an outsider might see them; he cannot, like Burns in *Tam o'Shanter*, project his reader into the mind of a peasant'.[5] A letter to Allan Cunningham makes it clear where Clare felt his own literary allegiances lay.

> He [Bloomfield] is in my opinion our best Pastoral Poet. His 'Broken Crutch', 'Richard and Kate', &c. are inimitable and above praise. Crabbe writes about the peasantry as much like the Magistrate as the Poet. He is determined to show you their worst side; and, as to their simple pleasures and pastoral feelings, he knows little or nothing about them compared to the other, who not only lived amongst them, but felt and shared the pastoral pleasures with the peasantry of whom he sung.[6]

By associating himself ('The Northamptonshire Peasant') with Bloomfield (whose trade as a shoemaker had proved an easy target for Byron's satire), Cunningham ('The Nithsdale Mason'), and James Hogg ('The Ettrick Shepherd') Clare gives some idea of the literary 'school' in which he would accept membership, a school free of the gentry attitudes (or 'moral weight') of Crabbe. To these we could certainly add the name of Burns. Clare declared, 'I would sooner be the Author of Tam o shanter then of the Iliad & Odyssey of Homer'.[7]

The example of Bloomfield is probably the most directly relevant to Clare's practice, and a number of the Suffolk poet's narrative poems can be compared to Clare's. Clare considered him 'the most original poet of the age & the greatest Pastoral Poet England ever gave birth too'.[8] His collection *Rural Tales* (1802) included, as well as 'Richard and Kate; or Fair-Day. A Suffolk Ballad', a poem that Clare particularly praised, 'Walter and Jane; or, The Poor Blacksmith. A Country Tale', 'The Miller's Maid. A Tale', and 'The Fakenham Ghost. A Ballad'. *Wild Flowers* (1806) included 'The Broken Crutch. A Tale', another poem singled out by Clare and one which figures in his own poem 'Opening of the Pasture', 'Abner and the Widow Jones. A Familiar Ballad', and 'The Horkey. A Provincial Ballad'. The framework of *May-Day with the Muses* (1822) is a rent day at which the local squire invites his tenants to pay their rents in rhyme. The narrative contributions are 'The Drunken Father', 'The Shepherd's Dream; or, Fairies' Masquerade', 'The Soldier's Home', and 'Alfred and Jennet'. Bloomfield remarked that the poems in *Rural Tales* 'treat of village manners, and rural scenes' (Preface). In the Preface to *Wild Flowers* he noted 'It will be observed that all my pictures are from humble life, and most of my heroines servant maids.'

That Clare should have been compared to Crabbe rather than Bloomfield is a symptom of modern assumptions with respect to the narrative poetry of this period. Karl Kroeber's survey of *Romantic Narrative Art*[9] mentions neither Clare nor Bloomfield. Hermann Fischer's account of *Romantic Verse Narrative* makes it clear why he has nothing to say about Clare. The genre he chronicles, what he calls 'the "romantic" metrical tale', is a phenomenon against which Clare was consciously reacting: 'a primarily narrative form, sensational or sentimental subject matter, a free range of metre, a wealth of colourful descriptions and an obvious striving for popularity'.[10] In one respect the comparison with Crabbe has point: Clare was trying as much as Crabbe to develop, in Fischer's words, 'an unromantic alternative to Scott's romances'.[11]

The Romantic fascination with the epic and the romance continues to bias the treatment of modern critics. Stuart Curran in his *Poetic Form and British Romanticism* devotes entire chapters to 'The Romance' and 'The Epic', while relegating Clare and Bloomfield as possible exponents of what he calls a 'Romantic georgic poetry' to a footnote in his discussion of 'The Pastoral'.[12] Signficantly, even in this brief mention he overlooks their practice of *narrative* pastoral.[13] The problem is not just that Clare is still considered 'minor' and thus neglected but that his place in the historical context remains problematic; in the Romantic period but not fully of it, his most distinctive and characteristic work is not well served by the critical categories that have been developed to deal with the works of Wordsworth and Coleridge or Shelley and Keats. Clare himself knew that his tastes were hardly in tune with the fashions of his age, and he complained

> this prolific age d[ea]ls in all sorts of out[landish ?] comoditys in gods goddesses sh[epherds] shepherdesses goths vandals & monsters of all sorts & [si]zes f[oreig]n witches of atlas the black & brown dwarf[s of] scots [sup]erstition but past[orals] the true pastorals seem to b[e left] badly off yet for Bloomf[ield] our "english theocritus" is laid bye & Wordsworth they [affect ?] to despise.[14]

Clare may himself have been trying to catch the taste of the time with a poem in Spenserian stanzas originally to be called 'the Deserter', which finally became 'Edmund & Hellen'. The subtitle of one version, 'or the Suecide', indicates Clare's desire to exploit the sensational possibilities of his story. Writing to Taylor under the pseudonym of 'Percey Green', he commented, 'I know a simple tale of love now a days...is nothing without at Castrophe mine is the "Suicide".'[15] Clare found himself thinking 'worse & worse' of this potboiler as he went, and modern readers might well agree.[16] The association of Wordsworth with Bloomfield is significant, since he is the only one of the major Romantic poets to practise, in poems like 'The Brothers' and 'Michael', the kind of pastoral narrative that Clare practised. We still have no satisfactory account of this kind of narrative poetry, and what follows is an attempt to sketch out some elements of such an account.

One suspects that identifiable literary antecedents may be less important to such poetry than a certain conception of the oral tradition. They are *tales* in that the telling (the *narration* in modern critical terminology) is as much the focus as the actual incidents recounted (the *histoire*). Of the ten tales included in this volume four ('The Two Soldiers', 'Valentine Eve', 'The Sorrows of Love', and 'The Memory of Love') are specifically told by someone whose narrative act is the object of imitation. Three more are dialogues ('The Rivals', 'Opening of the Pasture', and 'Jealousy'), in which the participants act as narrators as well as disputants. Clare saw a clear continuity between the oral narratives to which he had listened himself and his own narrative productions. At the time he was working on 'The Lodge House' he wrote to Octavius Gilchrist 'I am now Ryhming some of my Mother's "old Stories" as she calls 'em they are Local Legends Perhaps only known in these Places As my enquiry as never gained any hints of 'em elsewhere'.[17] His 'unletterd Parents' were also the source of 'Robs Terrors of Night'.[18] Clare was naturally delighted on reading Percy's *Reliques of Ancient English Poetry* (1765) to find 'all the stories of my grandmother & her gossiping neighbours . . . versified in these vols'.[19] We know that a number of Clare's narrative poems derived from local stories. 'The Fate of Amy' was based on a 'story . . . popular in the village',[20] and Clare passed on to Holland the original version as he had heard it 'related . . . by an old Woman'.[21] Significantly Clare made a conscious choice between the different oral versions available to him, rejecting the one he believed closer to the facts, because it 'crampt the Imagination (truth in my opinion in poetry always does)'.[22] Another poem about suicide, 'The Cross Roads or Haymakers Story', was based on a story that Clare had listened to 'from the simple old grannys of the village'. It is in this poem that Clare first dramatises the act of telling, allowing the 'simple old grannys' to supply him not only with a subject but also with a way of telling. As he himself puts it, 'I have preservd all their simplicity I coud by putting it in their mouths to tag in ryhmes'.[23] The same procedure is used in 'The Workhouse Orphan' with increasing flexibility, in that no introductory scene setting is employed to present the narrator to us, who is thus allowed to introduce himself and his subject simultaneously.

A comment on 'The Fate of Genius' shows how conscious Clare had become concerning his narrative technique: 'I mean for the Parish Clerk to be the relation'.[24] He is far from merely transcribing the 'Gossip Tales'[25] of his native village. Rather they provided him with a model of narration which he was able to apply to material from a variety of sources. 'Crazy Nell' was drawn, according to Clare, from a report in a local newspaper, though his editors have not been able to track down the source.[26] The plot of 'Valentine Eve' was supplied independently by Edward Drury and by John Taylor (see below, Part III), but Clare transformed the basic hint by having the story told by 'a gossip'[27] as an appropriate story for the day on which she tells it. In this tale, as in 'The Sorrows of Love' he takes full advantage of the opportunity to characterize the narrator, so that their feelings and reactions to the story they are telling are as important as the events themselves. In both cases the narrators were friends and companions of the central characters, personally interested in their fate but at enough distance to allow of some narrative objectivity. Not an entire objectivity, of course; the narrator of 'Valentine Eve' still remembers Kate's failure to honour her promise of a new gown on her wedding day! The involvement of the narrators (even stronger in the dialogue poems) lends the stories a double interest: not just what happened, but what did it mean to those involved or associated, and how well have they understood it?

Not all the readers of the time, even sympathetic ones, would have been likely to grasp what Clare was doing. Lamb complained to Clare about what he considered an excess of 'provincial phrases' in his poetry, and proposed Shenstone as an example: 'The true rustic style, the Arcadian English, I think is to be found in Shenstone. Would his Schoolmistress, the prettiest of poems, have been better, if he had used quite the Goody's own language?'[28] Clare, as it happens, had answered this very question by anticipation.

> Shenstone is a Good Poet but his pastorals (as I think) are improperly call'd so the rural names of Damons Delia Phillis &c & rural Objects Sheep Sheepfolds &c &c are the only things that give one the slight glimps of the Species of Poetry which the Title claims

> – Putting the Correct Language of the Gentleman into the mouth of a Simple Shepherd or Vulgar Ploughman is far from Natural –[29]

Clare has in mind Shenstone's 'A Pastoral Ode' and 'A Pastoral Ballad' rather than his 'The Schoolmistress'. Nevertheless, he might well have considered 'the Goody's own language' to be preferable to 'the Correct Language of the Gentleman'. Compared with a Coleridge or a Shelley Clare appears a rather simple-minded literary theorist – or a refreshingly blunt one. His assumption that a subject should be treated in its 'Natural' language could in any case be defended on the respectable neo-classical ground of decorum. His practice in his tales suggests a more subtle awareness that events occur within a whole moral context that must be expressed in its own language.

The appeal of Clare's tales is indeed more subtle than it might at first seem. After early shockers like 'The Fate of Amy', 'The Cross Roads', and 'Crazy Nell' (which Clare reckoned was likely to appeal to the taste of 'most novel readers'[30]) his mature tales are largely lacking in incident. John Taylor observed 'I dare say you will make a good Story of Jockey & Jenny – but to me the Plot seems to want Incidents – It is however the Art of Poetry to invest the simplest Story with all kinds of agreeable Associations so that the *Facts* are of minor Importance'.[31] Clare seems to have acted on principle here. His friend and literary advisor, Eliza Emmerson, herself a poet, replied to a lost letter from Clare: 'In reply to your opinions respecting "Action & Incident" – they should certainly be *Volunteers* – and, the interest & delicacy of a poem, may be totally destroy'd by crowding it with such Matters...'[32] When he was urged to get more 'action' in his poems he responded by remarking

> I think many of the productions of the day that introduce action do it at the expense of nature for they are often like puppets pulled into motion by strings & there are so many plots semi-plots & demiplots to make up a bookable matter for modern taste that its often a wonder how they can find readers to please at all.[33]

In deliberately shunning the advantages of incident and excitement

Clare was, whether consciously or not, following in the footsteps of Wordsworth, who pointed out what distinguished his own works 'from the popular Poetry of the day; it is this, that the feeling therein developed gives importance to the action and situation and not the action and situation to the feeling'.[34] The reactions of readers to Clare's tales is significant here, for it is precisely the emotional impact that they stress. 'Perhaps you will call me "a silly old woman" –' wrote Eliza Emmerson, 'when I tell you than [*sic*] I have shed many genuine tears of *sympathy* over *certain* passages of your "Village Stories" – they came home to my (what once was young) heart.'[35] The implication of a revival of earlier feelings in later age is also present in Elizabeth Gilchrist's comment that Clare might think her preference for 'Jockey & Jinney' and 'The Memory of Love' 'very like the choice of "sweet Sixteen" but I certainly at that age should not have felt the truth of your lines as I feel them now, & I remember those days as you picture them, "Memory gave them an eternal stay". it is a beautiful thought'.[36]

Despite reservations about what he considered his 'affected fooleries', Clare was an admirer of Wordsworth, whom he preferred to Crabbe.[37] Another passage from Wordsworth's famous Preface describes well what Clare was trying to do in his tales – in some respects it arguably describes Clare's practice more accurately than Wordsworth's own:

> The principal object then which I proposed to myself in these Poems was to make the incidents of common life interesting by tracing in them, truly though not ostentatiously, the primary laws of our nature: chiefly as regards the manner in which we associate ideas in a state of excitement. Low and rustic life was generally chosen because in that situation the essential passions of the heart find a better soil in which they can attain their maturity, are less under restraint, and speak a plainer and more emphatic language; because in that situation our elementary feelings exist in a state of greater simplicity and consequently may be more accurately contemplated and more forcibly communicated; because the manners of rural life germinate from those elementary feelings; and from the necessary

> character of rural occupations are more easily comprehended; and are more durable; and lastly, because in that situation the passions of men are incorporated with the beautiful and permanent forms of nature.[38]

Clare of course could never have been so conscious and calculating in his choice of poetic material. But we should not fall into the trap of assuming that he adopted his subjects, forms and language unthinkingly or without artistic distance.

Clare can be seen historically as poised uneasily between two cultures, the oral culture of his native village and the literate culture to which as a writer he aspired. Unlike a gentry poet such as Crabbe or Shenstone, the oral narrator participates in the same system of values and the same social practices as his or her protagonists. It would be a mistake to confuse Clare with the purely oral narrators whose practice he imitates, although his own tales were certainly available for subsequent oral transmission.[39] There are important similarities, but also important distinctions that need to be made. Oral narrators were above all the custodians of a collective memory, a function as much under attack as the rest of their way of life. Indeed, the ways in which the members of a small community understand and record the experiences of their fellows is itself an essential part of their way of life. As E.P. Thompson remarks, 'Traditions are perpetuated largely through oral transmission, with its repertoire of anecdote and of narrative example'.[40] Thompson has coined the term 'customary consciousness' and applied it to Clare.[41] But while Clare did see his poetry as possessing a memorializing function, we must see it as designed to commemorate rather than perpetuate a communal way of life. Upon inspection a good deal of the village manners recorded in his poetry belong to pre-enclosure days rather than to the time of writing and are thus beyond rescue in terms of practice. It is no accident that virtually all of the passages describing local customs in his pastoral poems can be paralleled in the letter that he wrote to Hone's *Every-Day Book* (Appendix II). Publications like this and *Time's Telescope* catered to a genteel curiosity about vanishing local customs; its contributors were in effect writing the epitaph of that culture which was for them the object of an alienated curiosity. If the oral culture has survived it is paradoxically because they were concerned to write it down, and Clare too was a writer and as such the custodian of a memory becoming divorced from social practice. An awareness of the distance between the genteel audience he addresses and the oral 'roots' of his poetry may be reflected in the way that Clare's narrators often deliver their stories to inattentive or uninterested auditors. The audience may of course be uninterested because they are aware of the ulterior motives of the narrators; in this context tales are rarely told for their own sake, but rather to make a point or enforce a moral, and often in the context of a debate, whether explicit as in 'The Rivals', 'Opening of the Pasture' and 'Jealousy', or implicit.

II

The centenary of Clare's death saw the publication of a new edition of *The Shepherd's Calendar*,[42] but it was an edition of the descriptive poems for the months, and it excluded the 'Village Stories' and the other poems that had been present in the original edition.[43] For the omission of the village stories the editors of the 1964 edition were called to task by some reviewers who thought that the original plan for the book ought to have been restored. The problem was, and is, however, to decide what the original plan was. In this bicentenary year of Clare's birth, 1993, it has been decided to publish both a new and corrected edition of the descriptive poems[44] and this volume which includes the four verse tales of the 1827 edition – 'Jockey and Jenny; or, the Progress of Love', 'The Rivals', 'The Sorrows of Love', and 'The Memory of Love, or the Soliloquy of Robin' – together with some other verse tales deriving from the same period, and reflecting a similar inspiration.

Even before the publication of his first volume, *Poems Descriptive of Rural Life and Scenery* in January 1820, Clare and his advisors had begun to plan his future literary projects. The initial suggestion for the book that was to become *The Shepherd's Calendar* (his third volume, published in April 1827) was summarized by John Taylor, Clare's publisher, as follows:

My Advice then was, that you should divide the Week's Employments into the 7 Days, selecting such for each as might more particularly apply to that Day, which is the Case with some of the Occupations; – that the remaining which might be pursued on any Day should be allotted so as to fill up the Time; – that the Sports, & Amusements should in like manner be apportioned out into the 7 Days; – and that one little appropriate Story should be involved in each Day's Description. – A different Metre might sometimes be introduced; for instance in the Tale, if it were supposed to be related by one of the characters of the Piece; or, otherwise the various Days might be marked by a varied Measure, but this would be as you thought best & found most agreeable to you. –[45]

Taylor may have been thinking of John Gay's *The Shepherd's Week* (1714) as a possible model; Clare certainly knew and admired Gay's work.[46] Taylor's suggestion that the tales might be told by particularized narrators suggests that he had appreciated a characteristic feature of Clare's narrative art, which was discussed in the first part of this Introduction. He was certainly not shy of giving Clare advice concerning his narrative poetry. Having read 'The Lodge House' he wrote as follows:

You must not mind my Criticisms, Clare, but *write away* – Only if you tell a Story again, like the Lodge House, don't let the Circumstances occupy so much of your Attention to the Exclusion of that which is more truly Poetical.... Poets do not tell Stories like other people; they draw together beautiful & uncommon but very happy Illustrations, and adorn their Subject, making as much Difference as there is between a common Etching and a full painted Picture. – But I am sure you know very well [what] Poetry is, and I don't fear but that v[ery soon] your [ ]ces will prove it.[47]

We can see here from the outset potential disagreements about the properly poetical narrative treatment of a subject which may not be unconnected with the final abandonment of the initial plan for a volume intended to contain both narrative and descriptive poetry.

Taylor had in fact located what was to be a continuing problem for Clare: that of discovering a framework within which his talents could be deployed to best effect. Taylor shows some perceptiveness in his realization that such a framework was more likely to be in the nature of a compendium, built up of and comprising a variety of elements, rather than a single monolithic work. Not all of Clare's advisors were so perceptive. Edward Drury, the Stamford bookseller who introduced Clare to the notice of his cousin Taylor, actually kept back the letter in which Taylor first proffered his plan, anxious that it might distract Clare from the completion of 'The Peasant Boy', the poem that was eventually to become 'The Village Minstrel'.[48] Drury favoured ambitious works. He was, as we shall see, to offer Clare a subject for a work which he suggested could be modelled on Allan Ramsay's *The Gentle Shepherd* (1725), a five-act play. Such a work would, exulted Drury, no doubt because of its larger scope, be 'worth a score of "Weeks in the Village"'.[49] Here his sense of rivalry with Taylor is painfully clear. In the event Clare did treat the offered subject (which was also offered him independently by Taylor), but made of it no more than a tale, 'Valentine Eve', intended indeed to form part of the 'Week in a Village' project that Drury so scorned. Compared to his Romantic contemporaries Clare often seems strangely lacking in ambition – but perhaps he was wise to be sceptical of the more extended poetic forms then in vogue.

Neil Fraistat has rightly emphasized the importance that the collection as a unit had for poets in this period.[50] Clare in fact often approached his own work in a spirit of creative editorship, producing a whole series of notebook 'editions', complete with title-pages, in which he would select and arrange from his accumulated *oeuvre*, the most significant being *The Midsummer Cushion* (Peterborough MS A54), the only one actually to see print in the form that he himself envisaged, though it took a century and a half to do so.[51] It is thus not surprising that he recognized the advantages of the kind of plan proposed by Taylor, and he wrote to Taylor's partner, Hessey, 'I think a series of little poems connected by a string as it were in point of narrative woud do better then a canto poem to please critics'.[52] He explained that his 'Ways of a Village' – as he rewrote Taylor's original 'Week in a Village' proposal – would be 'a series of short Poems descriptive of the occupations in rural affairs. – Specimens of rural manners – & narratives of merrimental meetings at feasts fairs & weddings', and he asked Hessey to confirm that Taylor would indeed prefer this to 'a long connected poem in Cantos'.[53] Clare's rejection of what he calls a 'canto poem' – the kind of extended project that Drury seems to have preferred – implies a deliberate decision not to follow the fashion for lengthy romantic narratives, a fashion which (his reference to the critics suggests) he seems to think had in any case run its course.[54] But as Clare himself declared, 'I mind no fashions'.[55] We saw in part one of this Introduction how his own verse narratives were written in reaction rather than obedience to prevailing fashions.

The main problem with the 'compendium' structure proposed by Taylor and adopted by Clare was its lack of definition. The whole that was to make sense of the parts could only emerge by retrospect, after the production of the parts, and thus could have only a tenuous role in shaping them. In rejecting the 'Week' structure proposed by Taylor, Clare lost any clear structuring principle, and it was at a calamitously late date that the structure of a monthly calendar was provided to replace it. Thus Clare was left free to write individual works as the fancy took him, but the question of just how they would finally be integrated into a satisfactory single work was left unresolved. The fact that his publishers had the whip-hand in deciding just what of the material available would see print and that they were inevitably influenced by economic factors in making their decisions complicated matters even further.

As we trace Clare's work on the 'Ways in a Village' project we can see how unsettlingly fluid the situation was. By August 1820 he could write to Taylor:

> I am cobbling up some pastorals but dont know how I shall succeed I have done 4 or 5 & thought little of them – but a second reading has given me a higher opinion & encouragd me to proceed tis your long wishd proceeding 'Ways in a Village'[56]

Within a fortnight he told his friend Sherwill that he was 'busy with "ways in a Village"' and asked for 'hints for subjects'. He noted that he had already done 'Death of Dobbin', 'Rural Morning' and 'Sunday Walks'.[57] On 18 October he wrote to Hessey that he had 'finished the "Cross Roads" "Rural Morning" "Evening" "Rustic Fishing" & "Sunday Walks" towards the village job'.[58] The poems listed are the first six poems in a notebook now in the Pierpont Morgan library (MA 1320), a notebook that Clare had evidently set aside for the 'Ways in a Village' project; the title-page reads 'Village Scenes and Subjects on rural Occupations. By John Clare the Northamptonshire Peasant Author of "Poems on life and Senery" & "Rural Poems & Songs" Helpstone August 21 1820'. The contents of this notebook, which made the journey to and from London for Taylor's comments several times, are a good guide to the development of the project. By the end of 1820 Clare had begun to chafe at the task he had set himself. 'I get on cursd bad with ways in a village,' he wrote to Taylor on 14 December 1820, 'I find the thing too circumscribed & narrow for ones thinking always dinging at rural things wornt do & what I have done I can get no ones opinion off thats worth an ha'penny'.[59] Taylor encouraged Clare to send up any work on which he wanted advice, and assured him 'Don't on any Account trouble yourself with more of the Ways of a Village – I dare say there is alm[ost suf]ficient to make a respectable volume'[60]; and indeed, with what Taylor found in the notebook that Clare accordingly sent him, there was. As he prepared to send his work up to London, Clare announced, 'the Ways of a village I shall give in for other pursuits were I may have more liberty'.[61] On 21 December Clare announced 'On Saturday the "Ways of a Village" comes to London all the pieces that are corrected none else', and was soon urging Taylor 'only tell me my faults in long poems of the Ways in a village you last got'.[62] The 'Quarto' that Clare sent Taylor was the Pierpont Morgan notebook, which at this stage contained the six poems that Clare mentioned to Sherwill and Hessey and also 'The Widow or Cress Gatherer'. As we now have it the notebook contains the following poems:

Rural Morning (pp.1-6)
The Cross Roads or Haymakers Story (pp.6-16)

Death of Dobbin (pp.16-21)
Rural Evening (pp.22-7)
Rustic Fishing (pp.27-30)
Sunday Walks (pp.30-4)
The Widow or Cress gatherer (pp.35-9)
The Vicar (pp.40-6)
Jockey & Jinney or first Love a tale (pp.47-68)
Wanderings in June (pp.68-78)
The Workhouse Orphan A Tale (pp.78-84)
The Fate of Genius a Tale (pp.84-9)
Pastime in Summer (pp.89-92)
The Last of Autumn (pp.92-8)
Maggys Repentance (In Continuation to "Robins Soliloquy") (pp.99-105)
Winter (pp.105-15)

Of these the first seven actually appeared in Clare's second collection, *The Village Minstrel*; Taylor in fact used all the then contents of the notebook for the edition in progress, which at this point he intended to entitle 'The Ways of a Village, with Songs, Sonnets, & other Poems'.[63] It was only on reading through 'The Village Minstrel' (or, as it was still called by Clare, the 'peasant Boy') that he decided to give it a central place and name the collection after it.[64] Clare acquiesced breezily in this plundering of the 'Ways in a Village' project: 'put all the pieces in the last Quarto in your new Vols which you think good . . . dont spare any thing for the 4th Vol – Ill be bound to have stuff enough by then'.[65]

With the publication of *The Village Minstrel* in September 1821 the 'Ways in a Village' project might seem to have reached its terminus. In fact, sending off what he had already completed to Taylor seemed to revive Clare's interest, and on 30 December 1820 he reported that he had 'begun the "Statute" a second time as a piece by itself & have several others for the ways in village now on the file so I shall have plenty for it without taking the old ones'.[66] Clare was soon announcing plans for poems called 'Days gone bye' and 'Loves of Jockey & Jinney'.[67] If the first is an alternative title for 'The Vicar', as is probable, then these are the next two poems transcribed into the Pierpont Morgan notebook.[68] Clare's interest was evidently turning in a narrative direction, and he told Taylor: 'I shall proceed next Spring with the string of rural Tales I at first intended – your Title will do I fancy'.[69] It is not clear what the suggested title was (presumably 'The Ways of a Village'), but Taylor certainly encouraged Clare to pursue his new direction. He admired 'The Cross Roads' and suggested to Clare 'another Volume of a more pensive Cast altogether – pathetic Narratives'. It is perhaps with an eye to this project that he suggested keeping back 'what was called "The first Pastoral" . . . for the sake of the Design you allude to of completing the Series at some future Time'.[70] Clare preferred the already completed pastoral to be included in *The Village Minstrel*, confident that he could produce fresh material for the new project, which certainly attracted him: '"Pathetic Narratives" I like much & shall muster up plenty of stories for that matter so spare & save for nothing'.[71] Mrs Emmerson encouraged him to proceed with his 'Pathetic Narratives', commenting that they 'will also afford you ample room to indulge in that, wherein you excel – In animated descriptions of Nature! heightend by the finer sensibilities of the Soul!'[72] By 17 May 1821 Clare had nearly finished 'The Vicar' which, he told Taylor, was 'one of those tales from your hint of "Pathetic Narratives".'[73] By 8 July he was less satisfied with this work (which he eventually incorporated into *The Parish*), but was planning 'The Workhouse' in which he would use material that Taylor had cut from 'The Cress Gatherer'.[74] 'The Workhouse Orphan', like 'The Vicar', was duly copied into the Pierpont Morgan notebook.[75] Meanwhile Hessey had proposed 'a Series of Village Sketches like some of those in the new Volumes' as 'interesting articles' for the *London Magazine*.[76] Clare thought they would be 'too serious for magazines' and might lose by prepublication.[77] Two months later, though, he was telling Taylor, 'I will begin a series of "Village Sketches" for the Mag: as Hessey hinted a while back'.[78] The original project for 'Ways of a Village', to consist of descriptions of local customs and of narratives, had hardly proceeded on a straight track; but it is still discernible in the double form of 'Village Sketches' and 'Pathetic Narratives'.

It seems to have been Clare who first thought of the 'plan of a Poem for each Month' which Hessey thought 'a good one' and Taylor 'a capital idea'.[79] Clare seems initially to have tried to compose seriatim with the progress of the year, publishing the results in the appropriate months in the *London Magazine*. In February 1822 he was contemplating 'April' and 'a short thing for March if possible'.[80] In early April he was losing faith in his intention to produce a 'May mornings walk', and thinking rather of a continuation of 'The Village Minstrel'.[81] He was still struggling with 'Walks in May' in May, but 'Wanderings in June' was already prepared in the Pierpont Morgan notebook, and was duly published in the *London Magazine* (in the July issue!).[82] The working title for this project was to become 'Summer Walks'.[83] The title can be found in one of two companion volumes (Peterborough MSS A29 and A30) into which Clare eventually copied much of the contents of *The Shepherd's Calendar*, and which are probably the two books that Taylor gave Clare in February 1822 as a successor to the Pierpont Morgan notebook, writing 'You shall have a Stand-Cart & a Go-Cart in these two MS. Books – one can come up here while the other is filling and then you shall have a fresh Supply'.[84] Drury was sceptical about the 'Summer Walks' project, noting that 'the subject does not appear to me from its title to be *very particularly* adapted for public notice'.[85] Another friend, Henry Cary, the translator of Dante, was more encouraging: 'From the specimen you send me I have no fear but your "Summer Walks" will be as faithful to nature & as much elevated by reflection as your poems have hitherto generally been'.[86] By November Clare had in fact shelved the project, with the possibility of renewing it 'next summer'.[87]

By 1823 matters were advanced enough for John Taylor to be talking in fairly definite terms about the new volume, and to propose a new arrangement which echoed Clare's plan of eighteen months earlier but raised more difficulties than it solved:

> I shall be very agreeable to the Publication of another Volume this ensuing Winter, & what with the [London] Magazine Poems & some long & good ones you have beside I doubt not a very creditable Volume may be completed without any great

Difficulty. Talking the other day with Hessey it occurred to me that a good Title for another Work would be – 'The Shepherd's Calendar' – a Name which Spenser took for a Poem or rather Collection of Poems of his. – It might be like his divided into Months, & under each might be given a descriptive Poem & a Narrative Poem – nay I don't know why the "last of March" & such like Pieces might not as well be introduced. But if you like the Thought we can easily settle a Plan.

It would do very well to call the next Volume by such a Name, adding "& other Poems" to take in such at the End as would not come well in under the Months. But such as Jockey & Jenney would find their Places under those particular Months in which the Story is laid. –[88]

Clare replied immediately to Hessey, Taylor's partner, saying that he was pleased with the proposed title of the new book but adding 'I fear T[aylor] indulges too great expectations on my new M.S.S. which he has not yet seen'. In particular he was worried that he would not have a verse tale to accompany each month, though 'I coud soon daub pictures anew for the Descriptive'.[89] We have no further relevant correspondence until Hessey's letter of 13 October 1823 which acknowledges the receipt of 'the Day Dream in Summer, Morning in the last of Summer – Spring – & the little Tale of the Grasshopper' and others. About these others Hessey is guardedly complimentary, saying that he can enjoy the descriptions because of his 'knowledge of the author, & my former familiarity with such scenes & objects', but adding: '(by the way I should relish them much more if you would bestow a little more pains on the writing, the mechanical operation of writing I mean).' He also remarks:

The descriptions however are too general to excite much Interest – there wants a human interest – a Story or a more particular delineation of character, and this might easily be given from the experience you must have had of life as well as from your own power of Invention or Combination.[90]

There seems to be emerging from such remarks a clue to the differences between Clare and his publishers. They were not in favour of pure descriptions of nature however faithful they might be. Taylor wrote to Clare some time later:

> I have often remarked that your Poetry is much the best when you are not describing common Things, and if you would raise your Views generally, & speak of the Appearances of Nature each Month more philosophically (if I may so say) or with more Excitement, you would greatly improve these little poems; some parts of the November are extremely good – others are too prosaic – they have too much of the language of common everyday Description; – faithful I grant they are, but that is not all – 'What in me is low, Raise & refine' is the way in which you should conceive them as addressing you . . .[91]

Taylor and Hessey wanted to get away from descriptive nature poetry and to stress human interest. Verse tales would clearly assist that intention because they would require a story with human actors. Even in the descriptive poems of *The Shepherd's Calendar*, they were looking for human interest and popular events such as were to become the meat of William Hone's *Every-Day Book* (1826-27). Hessey therefore suggested:

> The Shepherds Calendar should consist of delineations of the face of Nature, the operations of the husbandman, the amusements, festivals, superstitions, customs &c of the Country, and little stories introduced to illustrate these more accurately and to fix an Interest on them.[92]

Perhaps one might cynically describe this as a recipe calling for a mixture of *Old Moore's Almanac* and *Woman's Own*. There is no doubt that Clare tried to respond. The descriptive poems of *The Shepherd's Calendar* include many descriptions of 'amusements, festivals, superstitions, customs &c', as well as a survey of the farming activities of each month, and delineations of nature. Generally speaking the landscape of *The Shepherd's Calendar* is a landscape filled with human activity. The verse tales, on the other hand, are stories of common human interest – disappointed love, humble girls finding rich husbands, brave soldiers defending frightened maidens. Nor is it necessary to suppose that Clare was acting against his natural inclinations in dealing with such subjects. His culture was nothing if not popular – rooted in folk-song and folk-story, in newspaper accounts of domestic tragedy, and in the stories told by weeding-women during heavy showers. He enjoyed reading almanacs and Hone's *Every-Day Book*: he adored chapbooks and broadsheets.[93]

Hessey put forward a more detailed plan for *The Shepherd's Calendar* than Taylor's, perhaps after discussion with his partner who was the guiding spirit of the *London Magazine*. In that journal, too, festivals were receiving special attention: 'Horace Smith was directly inspired in the writing of his 'Death – Posthumous Memorials – Children' by Lamb's essay "New Year's Eve". And the essay "The Praise of Chimney Sweepers" by Lamb himself was firmly derived from B.W. Procter's "On May Day".'[94] Hessey's plan similarly stressed such events:

January –	New Year's Day – Winter Sports – Skating &c
February –	Valentine's Day – a good subject for a Love story
March	First approach of Spring
April –	The Poem of Spring already written, with the addition of some little Story
May –	The Day Dream
June	Haymaking – an abundant theme for Stories
July	Sheep Shearing – the same
August –	Harvest beginning – (last of Summer
September	Harvest Home – a Capital Subject – describe a real Scene
October –	the last of Autumn – Field Sports – Story
November –	Dismal feelings on the Approach of Winter Pathetic Story
December –	Frost, Snow, Christmas Gambols Winter Sports – Miseries of the very poor – Story –[95]

Another later hand has made entries in the margin that seem to suggest 'The Memory of Love' for February and 'Jockey & Jenny' for June, but we have been unable to identify the hand and cannot suggest a date for these insertions.

Thereafter Clare continued to adhere as much as possible to Hessey's and Taylor's schemes for *The Shepherd's Calendar*. When he first received Hessey's plan, he had already done some work and was a little put out not to have been informed earlier of Hessey's proposals.[96] He also did not agree with Hessey's endorsement of 'The Day Dream' as 'a good Specimen of what the thing might be – it contains a pleasant description of the face of Nature & it has a [ripe ?] strong and beautiful human Interest – it is the best in the book –'.[97] Clare said: 'I reckoned the Day-dream nothing nor can I think much of it now'. The poem is autobiographical, describing in rhymed couplets his reveries about his childhood, his first love for Mary Joyce, and then the fading away of his dreams of their continuing relationship. It is a better poem than Clare suggests, but it did not fulfil his hopes and expectations of what he might achieve in pastoral. One can see, however, why Hessey might be pleased with 'The Day-dream'. 'New scenes' that 'appeard in fairy light' replaced a 'reality' that 'seemed fading by'. The dream form accordingly gave the natural scenes a legitimacy in Hessey's eyes that he was unprepared to recognize in Clare's more straightforward descriptive verses. Childhood, too, was an acceptable subject, and first love that was little more than fantasy was more acceptable than village slap-and-tickle. Hessey said plainly that the poem about Helpstone Statute Fair would not do, probably because it was not 'romantic', not 'idealistic', but rumbustious and earthy.[98]

One should remember that the verse tales of *The Shepherd's Calendar* period were not Clare's first attempts in this genre and Taylor's taste had not accorded with his own on previous occasions. Both 'The Lodge House' and 'Crazy Nell' had been written to satisfy Taylor's requests for something that would be both terrific and pathetic, that would, in fact, compete with the growing vogue for the novel. There is a note in Clare's hand mentioning a number of verse tales that he wanted to include in *The Shepherd's Calendar*, including two, 'Death of Dobbin' and 'The Poets Grave', which were of earlier vintage.

I shall have these inserted in the New book
Death of Dobbin   lost by T[aylor]
Robins Soliloquy   lost by T[aylor]
Maggys Repentance
Jocky & Jenny

Valentine Eve
The Poets Grave
The Vicar
A Days Pastime in Summer[99]

'Robins Soliloquy, or the Memory of Love', 'Jockey & Jenny' and 'Valentine Eve' we print in this volume. 'The Vicar' became part of *The Parish.*[100] 'A Days Pastime in Summer' is the poem called by Hessey 'The Day Dream', which became 'The Enthusiast' in *The Midsummer Cushion*. 'Death of Dobbin' and 'Maggys Repentance' were published in *The Early Poems of John Clare*, and 'The Poets Grave' is another name for 'The Fate of Genius', also published in the *Early Poems*.

Another of Clare's plans for *The Shepherd's Calendar* gives:

January is The Cottage Evening
Tale February – Sorrows of Love
March – Descriptive (long Book)
April – Spring
May – Descriptive 8:Syll[able]
June – [Memory of Love *deleted*] The Rivals & a
Descriptive Poem
July – Descriptive – 8:Syll[able]
August – D^{o} – ([Spenserian *Deleted*] Heroic)
Sept[ember] – Memory of Love an old Man's Tale
Oct[ober] –
November – Description (Spenserian)
Dec[embe]r – Christmas (short in Stanzas) 4to
Tales which may come in
The Rivals (abt July) [long Book]
Day Dream in Summer
Morning Walk 4to [101]

The second set of suggestions by Clare probably came at a fairly advanced stage in the development of the volume, because between this and Clare's earlier plan, 'The Vicar' and 'The Fate of Genius' had dropped out.[102] The second list mentions some new items. No trace of the composition of 'The Sorrows of Love' has survived, though it is probable that it is at least partly a response to Taylor's suggestion of 'Pathetic Narratives'. 'The Rivals' is probably the poem that Clare describes in a letter replying to Taylor's of 3 April 1824 as 'the Pastoral'.[103] Clare went on, 'if I live I intented to write 11 more in [that] way & had begun another "Love & Flattery".' The confused grammar reflects Clare's uncertain plans. Twelve pastorals suggests a deliberate attempt to fulfil the model of a 'Shepherd's Calendar'; but at the same time Clare wanted to believe that he already had enough for a new volume and was impatient to get it in the press. 'Love & Flattery' is the subtitle of 'Opening of the Pasture'. Clare more or less completed this poem and its companion, to which he gave the title 'Pastoral 2nd – Jealousy'. The second (which ends rather abruptly) has had to be pieced together from the incomplete fair copy in Peterborough MS B8 and the pieces that Clare had assembled in A50. The evidence points to a project in which Clare had lost interest, presumably at the point when the contents of *The Shepherd's Calendar* were decided on and it was clear that the new pastorals would not be needed.

Matters progressed in a state of frustrating flux. From the beginning of 1824 until his visit to London in May 1824 to consult Dr Darling, Clare was ill, spiritually and physically, and seems not to have been making much progress with *The Shepherd's Calendar*. He was, moreover, dismayed by the news of Robert Bloomfield's death in 1823, notified to him by Thomas Inskip some time before 10 August 1824:

> – I heard of Bloomfield's death & it shocked my feelings poor fellow you say right when you exclaim 'who would be a poet' I sincerely lovd the man & readily (nay gladly) acknowledge his superiority as a Poet in my opinion he is the most original poet of the age & the greatest Pastoral Poet England ever gave birth too –[104]

This reminder of Bloomfield just as he was in the process of assembling tales or 'pastorals' for *The Shepherd's Calendar* is important. In the letter to Hessey of 13 October 1823, Clare had written a review of English pastoral poetry (see Appendix III) in which he said: 'the true pastorals seem to b[e lef]t badly off yet for Bloomf[ield] our "english theocritus" is laid bye & Wordsworth they [affect ?] to despise...' Now, in September 1824, Clare wrote to Allan Cunningham: 'I beg your acceptance according to promise of the autograph of our English Theocritus, Bloomfield. He is in my opinion our best Pastoral Poet. His "Broken Crutch", "Richard and Kate", &c. are inimitable and above praise.'[105] Clare was reading very widely in English pastoral poetry at this juncture, often among poets who have since been forgotten – Robert Noyes (1730-98), William Crowe (1745-1829), Thomas Brerewood (d.1748), William Woty (1731-81), Richard Graves (1715-1804), and others – but it was still Bloomfield who held pride of place. Meanwhile Clare was also trying to retrieve his manuscripts from Taylor and in March 1825[106] even prevailed upon his friend, T.E. Artis, to call upon Taylor in London, all to no avail. He was still mourning Bloomfield in March 1825 and praising his *Farmer's Boy*.[107] In April 1825 Clare brought the quarrel with Taylor to a head and the correspondence between the two men in this and the next month was heated. It had the result, however, of focusing Taylor's mind on the completion of *The Shepherd's Calendar* for the press.

Unfortunately Taylor complained that he now had too much material for the volume:

> I have been reckoning the number of Lines and Pages which the present plan of our next Volume gives us and I find we shall have about twice as much Matter as we require – 20 pages to each Month will make a Vol of 240 pages, which alone is a large quantity – now the Cottage Evening alone extends to 19 entire pages, – and the Sorrows of Love make 16: to join them both in one month will therefore swell the work out too much.[108] What shall we do? – Shall we put only one piece of Poetry under each Month? I don't know how we do otherwise. – In that case we will keep the Cottage Evening for January, and instead of the Verses descriptive of Febry we will insert the Valentine's Day alone, bringing the Sorrows of Love into March,[109] and omitting the Descriptive Lines here again. What think you of this? – There is a feeling of propriety in it I think, from the Character of the Stories, – but perhaps a very few Lines might be prefixed to each Story from the Descriptions –

> yet that would plunder them of their Sweets, and make a Sad Waste of your Labour. – Shall we insert the Descriptions only and leave the Tales for another Volume? 'Clare's Cottage Stories' would not make a bad title. – The most unlucky thing in such an arrangement would be the diminished Interest of the Descriptive Volume if the Stories were separated, – and the comparative Sameness of the Pieces with some you have already published.[110]

Clare was naturally dismayed and wrote in his journal for 29 July 1825: 'Received a proof from Taylor – the plan is again altered & he now intends to print the Months only & leave out the Tales this plan is one that puts the worse first & leaves the best to a future oppertunity –'[111] Even that wasn't the end of the story. In December 1825 Taylor told Mrs Emmerson 'that *half* of it was *already* in *type* – that he proposed to publish one Vol with the *Months* and *close* the book with a few of the *Tales* – leaving the rest of the "tales" for a 2^{d}. Vol,'[112] which suggests an intention to include more than four of the tales. By July 1826 he was complaining that he now had too *little* material, and was asking Clare if he had another story that could be used![113]

As we know, *Clare's Cottage Stories* never appeared. In *The Shepherd's Calendar; with Village Stories and other Poems* (London, 1827), four verse tales were published: 'The Sorrows of Love; or, the Broken Heart' (pp.103-18), 'Jockey and Jenny; or, the Progress of Love' (pp.119-45), 'The Rivals; a Pastoral' (pp.146-66) and 'The Memory of Love; a Tale' (pp.167-81). The rest disappeared into Clare's capacious rag-bag, two being included in Clare's compilation, *The Midsummer Cushion*. Clare had therefore undertaken a great deal of work for the first edition of *The Shepherd's Calendar* for which he received no remuneration and no recognition. Yet, throughout the long gestation of *The Shepherd's Calendar*, Taylor and Hessey had pushed the verse tales in preference to the descriptive verses. Taylor continued to criticize the descriptive verses, forcing Clare to rewrite 'July' entirely and saying of 'November': 'some parts . . . are extremely good – others are too prosaic – they have too much of the language of common every-Day Description'.[114] Gradually even Clare himself had been persuaded that the verse tales were important.[115] But in the end the descriptive verses took pride of place. Even the choice of verse tales that were published did not represent Clare's preference. He particularly liked 'Valentine Eve' and told Taylor so.[116] Taylor ignored him. Finally, there was a switch in the public's taste. Hermann Fischer believes that the verse narrative, which 'between 1790 and 1830 represented a fashion trend', began to lose its appeal.[117] A contemporary, Christopher North, while reviewing James Montgomery's *Pelican Island*, concluded in October 1827 that, in general,

> Poetry... has long been a drug in the market – there has for many years been a glut of that commodity – nor will either wholesale or retail dealers, nor persons not in trade, on any account buy any sorts of it, even at the most reduced prices.[118]

Montgomery himself thought that 'poetry has had its day in the present age'.[119] Taylor reported to Clare: 'The Season has been a very bad one for new Books, & I am afraid the Time has passed away in which Poetry will answer. – With that beautiful Frontispiece of Dewints to attract attention, & so much excellent Verse inside the Volume, the Shepherd's Calendar has had comparatively no Sale.'[120] The long and frustrating delays in getting the volume out led to its publication at the worst possible moment. '...ryhmes is gone or going out of fashion for a season,' Clare lamented to De Wint, '& Mr Colbourns Novels by new unknowns & little great knowns coming in'.[121]

III

Having discussed how Clare's main narrative production emerged from the shifting plans leading to the publication of *The Shepherd's Calendar* and considered in general the kind of poems he was trying to write, we will now consider briefly the individual poems contained in this volume.

'The Lodge House' was a poem which Clare himself, and his village friends, liked very much. It is vigorous, even exciting; it is contemporary; it is full of humour and sly observation, and a true 'gossip's tale'. It was written in late 1819 from one of 'my Mother's "old Stories" as she calls 'em'.[122] Clare wrote to Captain Sherwill on 24 February 1820: 'the Lodge House I must confess this bit of pride is I think the best as it is the most original subject'.[123] Smarting a little from comments made about 'Solitude', Clare wrote to Taylor:

> my lodge house I think will be above your thumbs & Keats too it is [past] undergone the Critiscism of my father & mother & several rustic Neighbours of the town & all aprove it you will agree they beat your polite Critics in that low nature which you never prove but by reading & which them & I have daily witnessd in its most subtle branches[124]

Taylor was unlikely to be receptive to appeals to 'low nature', and he at first ignored the poem.[125] When he did offer his comments he remarked that 'as a Story this of Lodge House may appear to all your Hearers capitally told, and yet that it has not the Superiority about it which makes good Poetry'.[126] On 6 November 1821 Clare offered it to the *London Magazine* and suggested that Taylor might publish it anonymously, to no avail.[127] One suspects that Taylor's objections were not purely aesthetic. Like 'Helpstone Statute', the poem was overly vulgar for the genteel taste of Clare's advisors. Mrs Emmerson thought that 'tho very clever, it does not suit my taste; nor to own the truth, do I think such subjects, worthy of your Genius!', and she wished that Clare would 'soar to the loftier regions of poesy'.[128] Clare still thought well enough of the work to copy it into Peterborough MS A40, though this later version shows some sign of being revised to meet polite taste half-way, and we have preferred the early fair copy in Peterborough MS B2.

The story behind 'The Two Soldiers' is remarkably like that told in 'The Lodge House' and it seems probable that it is the same as the 'Soldiers Return' which Clare announced to Taylor as being, along with 'The Lodge House', 'Ready for your Inspection'.[129] Clare actually produced two verse versions of the story as well as an unfinished prose version. The version in pentameter couplets is itself unfinished, though most of it can be pieced together from the passages that Clare copied into Peterborough

MS A44 under the title 'The Two Soldiers a Tale Or mysteries of providence'. We have here preferred to give the other version, an untitled reworking in ballad metre, in which Clare puts the story into the mouth of a village granny. This is found in a relatively late manuscript (Peterborough A59, pp.1-5).

Clare first mentions his intention of writing 'a "Poem" on another Self murder (as Amy) measured 10s Intituled "Cross Roads"' to Taylor on 17 January 1820.[130] Taylor thought 'the Title of Cross Roads appears to me a very good one as well as original'.[131] By October Clare had finished it and probably copied it into the Pierpont Morgan notebook which is the source of our text.[132] Taylor said of the poem 'It has affected me to Tears every time I have read it', and Clare agreed: 'the tale often touchd me as I heard it told from the simple old grannys of the village'.[133] Having ignored 'The Lodge House' Taylor was happy to include 'The Cross Roads' in Clare's second collection, *The Village Minstrel* (1821), and he singled it out in an article on Clare published in the *London Magazine* in November 1821.[134]

'The Memory of Love' appears to be the poem that Clare and Taylor habitually referred to as the 'first' pastoral. Taylor showed it to Keats who liked it, though Taylor was 'afraid it is not poetical or select enough in certain parts of the Soliloquy'.[135] The original title was 'Loves Soliloquy'[136] or 'Robins Soliloquy', under which it figures in one of Clare's lists of contents intended for *The Shepherd's Calendar*, where he recorded it as having been 'lost by T[aylor]'.[137] Despite Clare's protest it was omitted from his second collection, *The Village Minstrel*, but was one of the four tales included in *The Shepherd's Calendar*.[138] Clare particularly wanted this poem to be included, to the point of listing it by both titles.[139] Taylor too, despite omitting it from *The Village Minstrel*, declared that the poem 'is with me one of the greatest Favorites'.[140]

One of the fruits of Clare's announced intention in January 1821 to 'proceed next Spring with the string of rural Tales I at first intended'[141] was 'Jockey & Jinney or first Love a Tale'. He already had 'the "Loves of Jockey & Jinney" in contemplation on 2 January.[142] By April he could report 'I have got on a great way with the tale of "Jockey & Jenney"...'.[143] Taylor's comment on the plot of the poem on 1 May suggests that Clare had sent him further details concerning the poem.[144] Clare was having his doubts: 'I am in fear its no Poem', and he sent the 150 lines he had completed for Taylor's comments.[145] On 29 May he told Mrs Emmerson that the poem had been *'abated* by *circumstances'*.[146] Taylor's delay in offering his reactions meant that no more of the poem had been produced by August.[147] When he finally replied to Clare concerning the poem on 14 July 1821, Taylor wrote 'I ought to have told you long ago that I very much admired your Beginning of that Story as far as it goes' and on 7 August he wrote 'You never wrote any thing finer than the Description of Night in Jockey & Jenny'.[148] By November Clare could report 'I have finishd "Jockey & Jinney" "Wanderings in June" & a ne[w poem] the "Workhouse Orphan"..."The Fate of Genius" will soon be started'.[149] The four poems mentioned are all together in the same order in the Pierpont Morgan notebook (see above, p.xxii), and it is probably at this time that Clare copied them into the notebook. It may well be the 'M.S.S. book' that Clare sent to Taylor in January 1822. By this time he had overcome his earlier doubts: 'I think very much of "Jockey & Jenney" now its gone & fancy it one of the best Ive written'.[150] Taylor agreed, and later said that it was 'always a great Favorite of mine'.[151] Taylor and Hessey thought of printing it in the *London Magazine*, but in the end it was decided to be too long.[152]

The Pierpont Morgan notebook of poems that Clare intended for his 'Ways of a Village' included 'Maggys Repentance', with the subtitle '(In Continuation to "Robins Soliloquy")'.[153] This poem was included in one of Clare's lists of poems intended for *The Shepherd's Calendar*.[154] In the event it was not included in that volume, and neither was 'Going to the Fair' which is actually a reworking of 'Maggys Repentance'. 'Going to the Fair' was included in *The Midsummer Cushion*. We have no further details concerning its composition. The title that Clare finally chose may have something to do with the fact that in 1828 his friend Rippingille painted a picture with the same title.[155] This was evidently a genre piece rather than a narrative picture, but either the poet or the painter (and one suspects the former) may have chosen the title as a deliberate homage to the other. When we compare the two versions of 'The Two Soldiers', one an impersonal narrative in pentameter couplets and the other a dramatized narrative in ballad metre, with the pair formed by 'Maggys Repentance' and 'Going to the Fair', the first a poem in octosyllabics dominated by Maggy's own soliloquy and the second an impersonal narrative in pentameter couplets again, an intriguing possibility emerges. Was Clare deliberately producing two versions of these poems, one popular in metre and explicitly rooted in oral narrative, the other more 'respectable' in metre and narrative perspective? If so, his final preference seems to have been for a form that combines features from both models. Clare first refers to his use of the pentameter couplet in a letter of 17 January 1820, where he announced he was planning to write 'The Cross Roads' in 'measured 10s'.[156] By October he was writing, 'how do you lik my uniform measures of tens I have got usd to it & cannot break myself of it',[157] and in January 1821, 'I like the "all ten" measure best of any now & shall keep on wi't doubtless they will next say in so doing I imitate Crabb...'.[158] What Clare did not borrow from Crabbe was the latter's impersonal and distant narrative perspective.

The most resoundingly successful combination of the pentameter couplet and oral narrative is to be found in 'Valentine Eve', which Clare particularly wished to include in *The Shepherd's Calendar* but which Taylor unaccountably omitted. Clare was to give it pride of place as the first of the 'Tales' included in *The Midsummer Cushion*. Taylor's failure to use it is the harder to understand in that it was Taylor who helped to give Clare the subject for the poem. The story in fact came to Clare in two versions sent to him, independently, by John Taylor and by Taylor's cousin, Edward Drury, which affords an interesting opportunity to see how Clare used his source material. One version was a fairly well-known real event, namely the courtship and marriage of the future Marquis of Exeter to Sarah Hoggins, who became known as 'The Cottage Countess'. The story was recounted by Hazlitt in *The New Monthly Magazine* for April 1822, and versified by Thomas Moore ('You remember Ellen', in *Irish Melodies*) and later by Tennyson in 'The Lord of Burleigh' (published 1842).[159] Clare's source is the obituary of the Countess in the *Monthly Magazine* (1797), which was brought to his attention by Edward Drury, who wrote:

If you would like to venture on a Dramatic Poem like Allan Ramsay's Gentle Shepherd, I could furnish you with an admirable Plot, founded on a real occurrence, highly poetical & suitable for that species of poetry – it is the actual circumstance of our present Marquess of Exeter's grandfather marrying a country girl of humblest life: the story is beautiful in plain prose & would be delightful in your rhymes, which would be employed on your favourite subjects of virtue, beauty, worth, in obscurity, & advanced through their merits into high rank. Read over Allan Ramsay's Gentle Shepherd again & observe how simple is the plan: do not divulge the hint till I can mature it for your use – but tell me soon if you are capable of making use of it. The Earl lived obscurely for a considerable time in the Village – courted the girl as a plain rustic – his circumstances & refined manners caused him to be doubted – some thought him a concealed robber, some a spy, some a coiner – yet he wooed the girl; & a year afterwards returned to Burghley house she conceived she was going to live as a kind [of] menial until the attendants undeceived her next morning. The whole is very romantic & lively and I would not have any person but you make use of it for the world – it is worth a score of 'Weeks in the Village' – for the story will contain all the characters you could put in the 'Week' – rivals, friends, old men, young ones, back biters, slanderers, enemies – and all this *little world* could be displayed: and then the finale would be so good, so complete. I wish you would come over soon to discuss the thing with me.[160]

Clare replied in a lost letter evidently expressing doubts concerning his abilities to undertake a project on such a scale, in return to which Drury urged 'Begin the Gentle Shepher*dess* then without further fear or doubt' and promised to send further information as soon as he had it.[161] He kept his promise with a transcription of the obituary which we print as Appendix I. His deprecatory dismissal of 'Weeks in the Village' reflects a certain rivalry between Drury and Taylor for influence over Clare. It is therefore ironic (if it is really a coincidence) that Taylor was himself to propose to Clare a story in essentials identical to that offered by Drury:

> For the Beginning of the next Volume I think it wo^{d} be as well as to have a long Poem, it the better distinguish the Book. What think you of something like the Gentle Shepherd, – a Dramatic Piece. I will try to think of a Story for it. I remember in a very respectable Farmers Family where I was acquainted, there was an exceedingly pretty Daughter called Lucy who to the Surprise of all her Acquaintance married a young Man who came to the House as a travelling Harvester – one of a band of Men who try to get Work by going round to assist the Farmers by getting in their Corn – and it came out afterwards that he was a rich Farmer's Son from Yorkshire who had taken that Course that he might see if he could anywhere meet with a Girl to his Mind – It would make with little Incidents a tolerably good Plot for a Tale.[162]

Like Drury, Taylor thought the story would make a good foundation for a dramatic work. In fact Clare did mention a '"Dramatic Pastoral"' among the 'projects' he announced to Mrs Emmerson in early 1822; this was to be called 'The Misterey', presumably in reference to the identity of the lover.[163] Clare seems to have begun work on the poem as we have it in late 1823, though Hessey thought the story had already been treated too often: 'the Marquis I am not so sure of – it has already been made into a Novel, and I think a poem also – has not Crabbe taken it?'[164] On 3 January 1824 he told Taylor that he had 'just finished' the tale.[165] On 3 April 1824, Taylor had still not read the poem, complaining that he found it difficult to read, 'but what I have seen I like, & I think the verses at the End are very tender & sweet'.[166] When the time came to decide on the contents of *The Shepherd's Calendar*, Taylor wrote, 'I have considerable Doubts whether anything good enough can be made of Valentine's Eve'; but his decision to omit may have as much to do with the fact that, as he went on to admit, he could not find the manuscript.[167] He had already asked Clare for it, who replied 'I have hunted over the M.S.S. & cannot find the Tale of "Valentine Eve" among them but I have a rough copy of it which I must make shift with'.[168] The finished version of the poem as we have it was probably a reworking from the rough copy subsequent to April 1826. Clare's narrative skill can be seen in his rejection of the more romantic elements offered by Drury (such as the future Countess thinking she was to be a menial – it would be a very suspect lover who played such mind-games with his future bride and Clare's suitor very properly reveals his true identity *before* offering marriage) and in enlisting elements from the possibly less authentic account of Taylor (such as the working as a harvester rather than merely being incognito, which characterizes the lover as a man with expectations who nevertheless wishes to know the farmer's trade from the bottom up rather than a genteel idler). Truth, Clare thought, always 'crampt the Imagination',[169] and he wisely resisted the temptations of truth that Drury's account offered.

Clare left the final preparation of the tales included in *The Shepherd's Calendar* to Taylor, commenting 'the "Tales" I think you can deal with better then I as they want nothing but pruning'.[170] What this could involve is clear from the case of 'The Sorrows of Love', originally entitled 'The Broken Heart'. In November of 1824 Hessey wrote to Clare:

> The best Poem in this collection is the Broken Heart, but it wants cutting down – the old woman is too garrulous – some of the touches are extemely simple & natural & they excite ones regret that there are not more of them – but if you look over the Poem you will see that the best parts of it are those relating to the poor girl herself or the old womans recollections of her own youthful feelings – . . . Suppose now you look carefully over the Story of the Broken Heart and try if you cannot prune and polish it down into a more perfect form[171]

In the 1827 version of 'The Sorrows of Love' over 220 lines (lines 3-4, 9-11, 24, 59-60, 63-76, 143-8, 171-4, 185-92, 195-228, 257-8, 269-72, 281-2, 295-6, 303-10, 321-2, 327-32, 357-8, 365-70, 377-82, 405-16, 429-40, 453-540, and 561-2) were omitted. It was probably with reference to this tale that Taylor commented 'I have been compelled to cut out a vast many lines'.[172] These excluded passages deal with such matters as the 'touchmenot', a stinging nettle hidden in a posy offered to girls to smell (lines 63-70); the offer of beer to village girls made by the loutish lover (lines 147-8); a protest against enclosure and the plight of the poor: 'Ere vile enclosure took away the moor / & farmers built a workhouse for the poor' (lines 173-4);[173] two passages about witchcraft (lines 185-92 and 202-28);[174] the mother's commonsense caution to her child; the custom of bringing fairings back for the children (lines 327-32); a joke about coffin-making (lines 407-16); the retribution brought to the lover by smallpox (lines 429-40); and a passage on the significance of dreams (lines 453-540). Part of the last passage (lines 472-540) was reworked by Clare as a separate poem, 'The Dumb Cake'.[175] In general, the effect of the omissions is to reduce just the very thing in which Clare was strong – his understanding of village customs and village behaviour. The tale therefore becomes more sentimental in its emphasis and that was just what the cockney taste of Taylor and Hessey preferred. They were, after all, catering to the metropolitan middle class, conservative in its politics and evangelical in its sentiments. No information concerning the composition of 'The Sorrows of Love' has survived, though it is probable that it is at least partly a response to Taylor's suggestion of 14 April 1821 that Clare should produce some 'Pathetic Narratives'. It was copied into Peterborough MS A29, probably at some time after February 1822, from which we have taken our text.

Clare's second list of contents for *The Shepherd's Calendar* includes 'The Rivals'.[176] A letter of 6 February 1824 from Mrs Emmerson to Clare reveals that Clare had told her of a plan to write twelve '*tales* of *Love*', of which he had 'accomplished' three; Mrs Emmerson confessed herself 'quite at a *loss to* judge, how you mean to introduce the 12 Months of the Year with your love-tales – making it "The Shepherds Calendar"'.[177] 'The Rivals' is probably the poem that Clare refers to in April 1824 as 'the Pastoral', announcing that he had thoughts of writing another eleven, of which 'Love & Flattery' was already begun.[178] 'Love & Flattery' is the subtitle of 'Opening of the Pasture', which like its companion poem 'Jealousy' and 'The Rivals' is a dialogue poem. This may give a clue to Clare's intention for the announced sequence of twelve poems; perhaps they were all to be dialogues, a form in pastoral writing that goes all the way back to Theocritus. As pointed out above, 'Opening of the Pasture' and 'Jealousy' barely exist in a completed form, and it seems likely that Clare was working on them at the time that the contents of *The Shepherd's Calendar* were finalized and that, with no obvious format for their appearance, he lost interest in continuing the project of twelve pastoral dialogues (one of which was appearing in *The Shepherd's Calendar* anyway). The copy texts for the first and part of the second are in Peterborough MS B8, which was a notebook into which Taylor and Hessey had poems in Peterborough MS A30 transcribed, probably in November 1824, before sending it to Clare, so the copy texts must be subsequent to this date.

Notes

1. Tim Chilcott, *'A Real World & Doubting Mind': A Critical Study of the Poetry of John Clare* (Hull: Hull University Press, 1985).
2. *The Poetry of John Clare: A Critical Introduction* (London: Macmillan, 1974), pp. 110-13.
3. *English Literature 1815-1832* (Oxford: Clarendon Press, 1963), p.134.
4. To John Taylor, 7 Jan. 1821; *The Letters of John Clare*, ed. Mark Storey (Oxford: Clarendon Press, 1985), p.137 (hereafter cited as *Letters*).
5. *Romantic Narrative Art* (1960; Madison: The University of Wisconsin Press, 1966), p.116.
6. 9 Sept. 1824; *Letters*, p.302. It is not clear which of Crabbe's works Clare has in mind here; his criticisms seem to apply most aptly to works like *The Village* (1783) or *The Borough* (1810), to which his own *The Parish* could be seen as a riposte. He mentions having read Crabbe's *Tales* (presumably the 1812 volume) and says he intends in his own fourth volume 'to have a good race with him', but goes on to remark 'when I read anything that gives me a hint I throw the book down & turn to it no more till mine's finished', which looks like a deliberate avoidance of what might have been a restrictive influence (to Taylor, 7 Jan. 1821; *Letters*, p.137). There is evidence that his view of Crabbe was not entirely negative; Drury, who admired 'Crabbe's sweet tales', was 'delighted' with Clare's 'spirited observations on Crabbe' (Drury to Clare, 9 May, 1821; Egerton 2245, fol. 316r).
7. *Letters*, p.437.
8. *Letters*, p.300.
9. See n.5.
10. Hermann Fischer, *Romantic Verse Narrative: The History of a Genre* (1964; Cambridge: Cambridge University Press, 1991), p.199.
11. Fischer, op. cit., p.126.
12. *Poetic Form and British Romanticism* (New York: Oxford University Press, 1986), p.237, n.42.
13. We use Clare's own preferred term of 'pastoral' for the kind of poetry he wrote, though its literal accuracy could be questioned. In so far as Clare's

rural world is one of communal labour and other activities, 'georgic' might well be a more accurate label.

14. Peterborough MS A46, p.93; see Appendix III.
15. 19 Oct. 1822; *Letters*, p.248.
16. To Hessey, 5 Nov. 1822; *Letters*, p.250.
17. Late Dec. 1819; *Letters*, p.24.
18. To Sherwill, 9 Feb. 1820; *Letters*, p.31.
19. To Hessey, 4 July 1820; *Letters*, p.82.
20. *John Clare's Autobiographical Writings*, ed. Eric Robinson (Oxford: Oxford University Press, 1983), p.102. The source may have been Granny Bains, a village cow-keeper.
21. *Letters*, p.13.
22. To I.K. Holland [mid 1819]; *Letters*, p.13.
23. *Letters*, p.183.
24. To Taylor, 6 Nov. 1821; *Letters*, p.218. By 'relation' Clare evidently means the relator.
25. *Letters*, p.31.
26. *Autobiographical Writings*, p.103; *The Early Poems of John Clare 1804-1822*, ed. Eric Robinson and David Powell (2 vols., Oxford: Clarendon Press, 1989), I.580.
27. Clare to Taylor, 3 Jan. 1824; *Letters*, p.288.
28. Lamb to Clare, 31 Aug. 1822; in Mark Storey (ed.), *Clare: The Critical Heritage* (London & Boston: Routledge & Kegan Paul, 1973), p.175.
29. To I.K. Holland, [mid 1819]; *Letters*, p.12.
30. *Early Poems*, I.579.
31. Taylor to Clare, 1 May 1821; British Library MS Egerton (henceforth cited as Egerton) 2245, fol. 314r (see *Letters*, p.187, n.1).
32. Mrs Emmerson to Clare, 21 Dec. 1821; Egerton 2245, fol. 397r.
33. To Taylor, 3 Jan. 1829; *Letters*, p.451.
34. Preface to *Lyrical Ballads* (1800), in Wordsworth and Coleridge, *Lyrical Ballads*, ed. R.L. Brett and A.R. Jones (London: Methuen, 1968), p.248.
35. To Clare, 15 Dec. 1826; Egerton 2247, fol. 240v.
36. To Clare, 29 Jan. 1827; Egerton 2247, fol. 261r-261v.
37. See *Letters*, pp.86-7, 371-2, 221.
38. *Lyrical Ballads*, pp. 244-5.
39. His friend Frank Simpson has left a vivid record of such a reading of 'The Memory of Love' (to Clare, 7 Dec. 1826; in *Clare: The Critical Heritage*, pp.198-9).
40. *Customs in Common* (London: The Merlin Press, 1991), p.8.
41. Ibid., p.180.
42. E. Robinson and G. Summerfield (eds), *John Clare: The Shepherd's Calendar* (Oxford University Press, 1964).
43. John Clare, *The Shepherd's Calendar, with Village Stories and other Poems* (London, 1827).
44. E. Robinson, G. Summerfield and D. Powell (eds), *John Clare: The Shepherd's Calendar* (Oxford, 1993).
45. Taylor to Clare, 21 Jan. 1820; *Letters*, pp.27-8. Taylor refers to 'a Plan which I had met with in your MSS. entitled a Week in a Village' (p.27); we have not

ourselves found this 'Plan'. Clare does refer to a piece 'either Written or now Writing' entitled 'Ways of a Village' (to I.K. Holland, [October? 1819], *Letters*, p.16), the title under which he habitually refers to the project inspired by Taylor's suggestion.

46. In a list of 'favourite Poems & Poets who went to nature for their images so that you may consult them & share the feelings & pleasures which I describe', Clare includes John Gay's *The Shepherd's Week* (1714) (Natural History Letter III, in *The Natural History Prose Writings of John Clare*, ed. Margaret Grainger (Oxford: Clarendon Press, 1983), pp.39-41). The nineteen volumes of *Cooke's Pocket Edition of Select British Poets* (1796-1808), item 163 in the Northampton Public Library collection of Clare's books, includes two volumes of Gay's works.
47. Taylor to Clare, 18 April 1820; Egerton 2245, fol. 90v-91r.
48. Taylor's original letter of 30 November 1819 makes it clear that Clare's plan had already mutated into what was to become 'The Village Minstrel': 'Among your plans was a Series of Poems to be entitled a "Week in a Village" – I think that is both a good Plan & a good Title – I believe you have altered it into long Poem in the Spenserian stanza, but if you have only done the Sunday part in that Measure, or but little more, & can divide the Occupations of the Week so as to fill 6 Days with different descriptions, and Incidents, relating the Occurrences of each in some *other* appropriate kind of Verse, I think you would form a work which could not fail to please much better than that long Poem – Think of it, & prepare your List of Country Occupations &c. for the respective Days, if you approve of it; & to make out the Interest of each Day introduce some fitting Story by way of Episode, or as an Illustration of some Sentiment which fell naturally in with your Description. –' (Northampton MS 44).
49. Edward Drury to Clare, 19 July 1820; Egerton 2245, fol. 180.
50. Neil Fraistat, *The Poem and the Book: Interpreting Collections of Romantic Poetry* (Chapel Hill & London: The University of North Carolina Press, 1985).
51. *The Midsummer Cushion*, ed. Anne Tibble and R.K.R. Thornton (Ashington & Manchester: Mid Northumberland Arts Group in Association with Carcanet Press, 1979).
52. 4 July 1820; *Letters*, p.82.
53. Early July 1820; *Letters*, pp.82-3.
54. The development and influence of the specifically Romantic verse narrative has been ably chronicled by Hermann Fischer in *Romantic Verse Narrative: The History of a Genre* (1964; Cambridge: Cambridge University Press, 1991).
55. *Letters*, p.82.
56. 31 August 1820; *Letters*, p.90.
57. 12 Sept. 1820; *Letters*, p.95.
58. *Letters*, p.107.
59. *Letters*, p.114.
60. 16 Dec. 1820; *Letters*, p.118
61. [18-20 Dec. 1820]; *Letters*, p.121.
62. To Taylor 21 Dec. 1820 and 2 Jan 1821; *Letters*, pp.123-4 and 131.
63. Taylor to Clare, 29 Dec. 1820; *Letters*, p.126.

64. Taylor to Clare, 6 Jan. 1821; *Letters*, pp.134-5.
65. To Taylor, [7 Jan. 1821]; *Letters*, p.136.
66. To Taylor; *Letters*, p.128. Clare had already treated the subject of the Statute fair in *The Village Minstrel*, stanzas 72-80 (*Early Poems*, II. 152-5). The separate poem 'Helpstone Statute' was finally included in *The Midsummer Cushion*. The phrase 'on the file' probably means 'being worked on'.
67. To Taylor, 2 Jan. 1821; *Letters*, p.131.
68. On 17 May 1821 Clare reported to Hessey 'I have nearly finished another its 'a tale of other days' I call it "the Vicar"' (*Letters*, pp.190-1).
69. 16 Jan. 1821; *Letters*, p.141.
70. 14 April 1821; *Letters*, p.182 nn.2 and 3. 'The first Pastoral' is 'Robins Soliloquy' or, as it was finally called, 'The Memory of Love'. Clare referred to this poem (which he called 'Loves Soliloquy') as 'the first pastoral' in a letter to Taylor of [7 Jan. 1821] (*Letters*, p.136). The fact that 'Maggys Repentance' in the Pierpont Morgan notebook is subtitled '(In Continuation to "Robins Soliloquy")' supports Taylor's assumption that Clare intended a series of such works.
71. To Taylor, 18 April 1821; *Letters*, p.182.
72. To Clare, 25 April 1821 (Mrs Emmerson erroneously wrote '1820'); Egerton 2245, fol. 96v.
73. *Letters*, p.195. In a missing letter of 29 May he apparently told Mrs Emmerson that 'The Vicar' was completed but that 'Jockey & Jenny' had been '*abated* by *circumstances*' (see Mrs Emmerson to Clare, 5 June 1821; Egerton 2245, fol. 325r).
74. To Hessey, 8 July 1821; *Letters*, p.203.
75. The present contents of the notebook had all been entered by December 1821, when Clare gave it to Drury to copy preparatory to sending it to Taylor (Clare to Taylor, 18 Dec. 1821; *Letters*, p.222). Drury's letter to Clare of 3 Jan. 1822 (Egerton 2246, fol. 269r; mistakenly dated to 1821) makes it clear that this is the notebook in question. Taylor had received 'the New Poems' by 1 Feb. 1822 (to Clare; Egerton 2246, fol. 11r).
76. 23 June 1821; Egerton 2245, fol. 330r (see *Letters*, p.201 n.3).
77. To Hessey, 26 June 1821; *Letters*, p.201.
78. 28 Aug. 1821; *Letters*, p.211.
79. Hessey to Clare, 4 March 1822 (Egerton 2246, fol. 32r, 33r).
80. To Taylor, 21 Feb. 1822; *Letters*, p.232.
81. To Hessey, 2 April 1822; *Letters*, p.235.
82. To Hessey, 11 May 1822; *Letters*, p.239.
83. See Clare to H.F. Cary, 23 Aug. 1822; *Letters*, p.246.
84. Taylor to Clare, 1 Feb. 1822 (Egerton 2246, fol. 11r).
85. Drury to Clare, 3 Aug. 1822 (Egerton 2246, fol. 96r).
86. H.F. Cary to Clare, 1 Sep. 1822 (Egerton, fol. 101v).
87. To Hessey, 5 Nov. 1822; *Letters*, p.250.
88. John Taylor to Clare, 1 Aug. 1823; Egerton 2246, fol. 228r-228v. There is an abbreviated version in *Letters*, p.278, n.3.
89. Clare to Hessey, *between* Friday 1 and Monday 4 Aug. 1823; *Letters*, p.282. For a time there was talk of calling the volume the 'New Shepherd's Calendar', first proposed by Hessey (to Clare, 6 Sep. 1823; Egerton 2246, fol. 238v).

90. Hessey to Clare, 13 Oct. 1823, Egerton 2246, f. 245v. The poems that Hessey mentions identify the volume he is referring to as Peterborough MS A30.
91. Taylor to Clare, 4 March 1826, Egerton 2247, f. 152.
92. Hessey to Clare, 13 Oct. 1823, Egerton 2246, f. 245v.
93. See E. Robinson, 'John Clare's Learning', *The John Clare Society Journal*, no. 7, July 1988, pp.10-25; 'John Clare and the Newspapers', ibid., no. 6, July 1987; 'John Clare and Weather Lore', ibid., forthcoming; and G. Deacon, *John Clare and the Folk Tradition* (London: Sinclair Browne, 1983).
94. T. Chilcott, *A Publisher and his Circle: the life and work of John Taylor, Keats's publisher* (London: Routledge & Kegan Paul, 1972), chap. 5, 'The London Magazine: 1821-5', pp.129-60.
95. Hessey to Clare, 13 Oct. 1823; Egerton 2246, fol. 245v.
96. Clare to Hessey, *after* Monday 13 Oct. 1823; *Letters*, p.286. This letter is not printed in its entirety in Mark Story's edition because it turns into an essay, later submitted to the *London Magazine* but not accepted; we print it as Appendix III.
97. Hessey to Clare, 13 Oct. 1823; Egerton 2246, fol. 246r.
98. 'The Statutes won't do – it is too coarse – you may be faithful in your pictures but you must not be too close in the resemblance of the coarsenesses of the clowns' (Hessey to Clare, 13 Oct. [1823], Egerton 2246, fol. 246r).
99. Peterborough MS B6, p.R78.
100. *John Clare: The Parish*, ed. with an introduction by E. Robinson and notes by D. Powell (London: Penguin, 1985), ll.1584-1787.
101. Peterborough MS A20, p.R41.
102. Writing to Taylor on 19 June 1825 he proposed dropping these poems as 'not applicable to the present title' and suggested using 'Valentine Eve' for February and 'Sorrows of Love' for March (*Letters*, p.333).
103. *Letters*, p.293. The full title of the poem in Peterborough MS A20 (pp.R26-R16) is 'The Rivals a Pastoral – July'.
104. *Letters*, pp.299-300.
105. Clare to Cunningham, 9 Sept. 1824; *Letters*, p.302.
106. See *Journal*, 31 March 1825.
107. Clare to Joseph Weston, 7 March 1825; *Letters*, pp.321-3.
108. This suggests that at this point 'The Sorrows of Love' was intended for January, whereas in Clare's plan (see above, p.xxix) it was allotted to February.
109. Still a *third* placing.
110. Taylor to Clare, 15 June 1825; *Letters*, pp.331-2.
111. *Natural History Prose Writings*, p.251.
112. Mrs Emmerson to Clare, 11 Dec. 1825; Egerton 2247, fol. 116v.
113. Taylor to Clare, 10 July [1826]; Egerton 2250, fol. 324r.
114. Taylor to Clare, 4 March 1826; *Letters*, p.363, n.2.
115. See Clare to Taylor, 27 Dec. 1825 and 1 Feb. 1826; *Letters*, pp.353 and 359.
116. Clare to Taylor, 27 March 1826; *Letters*, p.373.
117. *Romantic Verse Narrative*, p.x.
118. *Blackwood's Magazine*, No. 131. Cited in Fischer, op. cit., p.216.
119. To Clare, 7 Jan. 1828; Egerton 2247, fol. 387r.

120. To Clare, postmarked 3 Aug. 1827; Egerton 2247, fol. 322r-322v.
121. 14 Oct. 1827; *Letters*, p.400.
122. Clare to Gilchrist, [late December 1819]; *Letters*, p.24.
123. *Letters*, p.33.
124. 19 March 1820; *Letters*, pp.38-9.
125. Clare to Taylor, 19 April 1820; *Letters*, p.47.
126. To Clare, 18 April 1820; Egerton 2245, fol. 91r.
127. *Letters*, p.219.
128. To Clare, 10 May 1820; Egerton 2245, fol. 113r.
129. 17 Jan. 1820; *Letters*, p.26.
130. *Letters*, p.25.
131. To Clare, 12 Feb. 1820; Egerton 2245, fol. 37v.
132. To Hessey, 18 Oct. 1820; *Letters*, p.107.
133. Taylor to Clare, 14 April 1821, and Clare to Taylor, 18 April 1821; *Letters*, pp.182, n.3, and 183.
134. *Clare: The Critical Heritage*, p.164.
135. Taylor to Clare, 29 Sept. 1820; *Letters*, p.99.
136. Clare to Taylor, [7 Jan. 1821]; *Letters*, p.136.
137. See above, p.xxviii.
138. See Taylor to Clare, 14 April 1821, and Clare to Taylor, 18 April 1821; *Letters*, p.182 and note 2. Apparently the 'first pastoral' was actually set up and run off in proof during the preparation of *The Village Minstrel* (Taylor to Clare, 5 Dec. 1821; Egerton 2245, fol. 387v).
139. To Taylor, 28 Feb. 1826; *Letters*, p.363. See also Clare to Taylor, 27 March 1826; *Letters*, p.373.
140. To Clare, 7 Aug. 1826; Egerton 2247, fol. 202v.
141. To Taylor, 16 Jan. 1821; *Letters*, p.141.
142. To Taylor; *Letters*, p.131. He may have already been contemplating it in early December 1820, when he mentioned to Hessey a poem to be called 'the "Wedding"' (*Letters*, p.113).
143. To Taylor, 17 April, 1821; *Letters*, p.181.
144. See above, p.xiv.
145. To Taylor, 3 May 1821; *Letters*, p.187.
146. See Mrs Emmerson to Clare, 5 June 1821; Egerton 2245, fol. 325r.
147. To Taylor, 11 Aug. 1821; *Letters*, p.207.
148. Egerton 2245, fol. 343v, 352r.
149. Clare to Taylor, 6 Nov. 1821; *Letters*, pp.218-19.
150. To Taylor, 24 Jan. 1822; *Letters*, p.225.
151. To Clare, 8 April 1826; Egerton 2247, fol. 162r.
152. See Hessey to Clare, 30 Aug., 3 Oct. 1822 (Egerton 2246, fol. 97v-98r, 117r).
153. See above, p.xxii.
154. See above, p.xxviii.
155. Rippingille intended to exhibit it at Somerset House in 1828 (Mrs Emmerson to Clare, 4 Jan. 1827 [error for 1828] and 10 or 17 April 1828; Egerton 2247, fol. 252v, and Egerton 2250, fol. 169v).
156. To Taylor; *Letters*, p.25.
157. To Taylor, 3 Oct. 1820; *Letters*, p.102.

158. To Taylor, [7 Jan. 1821]; *Letters*, p.137.
159. See the headnote to Tennyson's poem in *The Poems of Tennyson*, ed. Christopher Ricks (2nd ed., 3 vols., London: Longman, 1987), II. 25. According to Hazlitt's account the young bride never recovered from the shock of finding herself the Countess of Exeter (*The Complete Works of William Hazlitt*, ed. P.P. Howe (21 vols., London: J.M. Dent, 1930-34), X. 25).
160. Edward Drury to Clare, 19 July 1820; Egerton 2245, fol. 180.
161. Drury to Clare, 24 July [1820]; Egerton 2250, fol. 158r-158v.
162. John Taylor to Clare, 5 Dec. 1821; Egerton 2245, fol. 388r-388v. Taylor was probably responding to an appeal by Clare for suitable stories; earlier in the same letter he wrote: 'I cannot recollect any Story of Interest connected with my early Days, except such as appeared in Books, or Ballads, and were the common Property of all the Country; but if I can learn or think of any Tale that seems likely to suit you I will communicate it The worst of it is most of such Tales turn upon Suicide after Seduction, and so they resemble your Cross Roads. –' (fol. 387r).
163. See Mrs Emmerson to Clare, 5 Feb. 1822 (Egerton 2246, fol. 18r), Clare to Taylor, 31 Jan. 1832 (*Letters*, p.228).
164. Hessey to Clare, 26 Dec. 1823; Egerton 2246, fol. 268v.
165. *Letters*, p.287.
166. *Letters*, p.291.
167. To Clare, 8 April 1826; Egerton 2247, fol. 162r. There is no extant manuscript of the whole poem earlier than the version in Peterborough MS A40, which probably post-dates this letter.
168. 27 March 1826; *Letters*, p.373.
169. See above, p.xii.
170. 28 Feb. 1826; *Letters*, p.362.
171. Hessey to Clare, 3 Nov. 1824; Egerton 2246, fol. 406r-406v.
172. To Clare, 31 May 1825; Egerton 2247, fol. 34r.
173. Clare included a version of this couplet in *The Parish* (lines 1692-3).
174. A recent article by J.L. Wood, 'A Crafty Science', in *Factotum*, No. 33 (March 1991), reveals the social context of fortune telling. Fortune tellers were particularly suspected of luring young women into prostitution; see J. Cruikshank's engraving on the back cover of this issue. Cf. Clare's story, 'The fortune teller', in Peterborough MS A46, pp.56-9.
175. Printed in Deacon, *John Clare and the Folk Tradition*, pp.70-2.
176. See above, p.xxix.
177. Egerton 2246, fol. 284r.
178. To Taylor, after 3 April 1824; *Letters*, p.293. The reference to marginal corrections suggests that Clare had sent Peterborough MS A20, the source of our text for 'The Rivals'.

The Lodge House

A Gossips Tale

On a heath stood a farm house as lone as coud be
Let em look where they woud nothing else coud they see
But here an odd furze bush & there an odd tree
    Green corn field & fallow land brown
More lonsomly too in a hollow it lay 5
The hermit like tennants no neighbours had they
To pop in & chat a few hours of the day
    Twas two mile or more from a town

The farmer was wealthy as many coud tell
He managd wi care & he ploughd his land well 10
& card not for living in such a lone cell
    If he coud get crops to his will
Of servants for labour he kept a good clan
Stiff chaps five or six & a sturdy head man
A house keeping maid & a under wench nan 15
    Who had in a dairey good skill

Who lives at a lodge but gen dangers prepard
So wealthy & lonly he kept a good guard
& four mettle bull dogs turnd loose in his yard
    & guns ready chargd for alarms 20
Twas nothing unlikley for rogues coming here
So noted for hurded up wealth as he were
The towns round about him for miles far & neer
    Had heard of his dogs & his arms

Tho nothing to scare em as yet hadnt been 25
Of any one tempting down right to get in
But folks lunging round it at night time was seen
    Which left em suspisions of fear
& maids often sed when the rest were gone church
That shagger-down fellows theyve seen on the lurch 30
That tryd at the front door & then at the porch
    & begd in excuse bread or beer

—O dear what sensations from solitude rise
What trifles she loves that a town woud despise
Een the squeakings of mice now the maidens woud prize 35
        & thus when alone theyd sit down
& listen the chirp of the sparrows to hear
& think em then songs of the linnet more dear
& all those fine singers in solitude drear
        As they put em in mind of a town 40

One day as it rather gets dusk at the hour
When the winters days done all it can about four
The thresher gave in & had cleand up his floor
        & took out the straw to the stock
When three lusty fellows peept into his barn 45
& the right road for somwere requested to learn
Tho drest like three clowns twas a blackis[h] conscern
        & the thresher was struck like a rock

They gun force discourse bout the master & men
What servants & dogs hed in keeping & then 50
Theyd squint i the yard & gin talking agen
        Poor michael he quakd like a leaf
He answerd their questions wi hah & wi no
But hinted on dogs & the guns for a show
For he had the deepness about him to know 55
        That such like woud frighten a thief

They then lungd away wi out bidding good night
Such tokens confirmd that his notions was right
Pleasd enough too were he to get out of their sight
        & instantly shut up his barn 60
& went to the servants & told 'em his doubt
Who cast their opinions & then gave it out
That men at that hour for no good came about
        Twas surely a hidden conscern

Be't een as it woud they got ready for work 65
To guard agen danger if peace shoud be broke
They hunted up cutting knife cudgel & fork
  & drove all the dogs in the house
Thus armd they were fixt let it be as it might
& doors they lockd up hard the windows shut tight 70
Each waited ast were upon thorns all the night
  & listnd as still as a mouse

Besure now & then mutterd hints went about
& fis'es were shook to note somthing without
Some fancyd a whistle some heard a shill shout 75
  & some heard their steps in the yard
Poor hog serving hodge frit to dead as it where
A'most dreaded the supper job going to draw beer
& dursnt go down i' the cellar for fear
  Wi out hed a dog for his guard 80

The wind whistld hollow the weather was foul
Round the jambs of the cottage the tempest did howl
The dog[s] rather restless gun grumble & growl
  & wagged their tails at the door
The candle curld winding sheets dismal to view 85
& tokening danger the fire burned blue
& plump to the maidens the coffin sparks flew
  Which made em neer sink on the floor

Footsteps pass the window! the bull dogs all bark
Theres one shouts for cudgel & one for a fork 90
& he take the gun who can best hit the mark
  & thus they are fixt for alarm
Som'at sorrowfull calls & the door gis a tap
Twas a voice like a womans — agen a small rap
Poor hodge he woud have it twas nought but a trap 95
  Tho the voice sed it meant em no harm

"Who ever ye be" said the master "begone"
Some bawld for the gun to let know they had one
& some tapt the bull dogs to harden em on
        & bragd of their savagness too   100
The door haunter woudnt wi little be scar'd
But still to come in begged terrible hard
It told em theyd little need keeping a guard
        Twas small harm a woman coud do

"The storm gatherd deep & my road got unseen   105
"Lost on the dark heath for an hour have I been
"My limbs are most stiffnd it freezes so keen
        "Id be thankful to lye in yer barn"
The master was tender it melted his breast
Who coudnt but pity a woman distrest   110
He instant called counsil to give her some rest
        Lord knows twas a shocking conscern

But hodge still presisted she meant em no good
The maidens both backd him "keep safe while they coud"
& vowd were they them let her wowl as she woud   115
        She neer shoud set foot i the lodge
"Most votes the day carried" wi caution & guard
A tall woman enterd the house the boy stard
The stranger een smiled to see him so scard
        & hard ran the jest upon hodge   120

Still he eyed her all over from top to the toe
& gogd wi his elbow the maids to let know
That her voice were to[o] gruff — women never talkd so
        Let the others consiet as they might
Quere fancys he couldnt get out of his head   125
As in crossing the house she seemd heavy to tread
'Sides her foot looked large — well he might go to bed
        But hed neer shut his eyes for the night

They questiond the stranger she answerd em well
Where bin & where going far as questions compell 130
But whod any sense in his head coud soon tell
    She were little to talking inclind
She woudnt go bed & good reasons were shown
Her fatherless childern all sleeping alone
She 'tended to start soon as first cock had crown 135
    For she coudnt be easy in mind

The head man knew well bout the place whence she came
& knew too as well there was none of her name
Had hodge or the maidens bin up to the same
    Theyd blobbd out the matter of course 140
He answerd her nothing but kept up his eye
& found hidden mistery lapt up in the lye
& wisperd his master the hint by & bye
    Who resolvd to scheme matters no worse

Bed time cometh on man & master sit up 145
The womans but vainly intreeted to sup
Poor hodge spite o fear begun drowsy & droop
    & she beggd theyd all go to their beds
For her part she wisht cause no trouble at all
The things that she begd of their kindness was small 150
& if she got worser she easy coud call
    —Excuse freshend doubts in their heads

So now left on garrison master & will
The woman they thought got uneasier still
But she said twas the thoughts of her babes made her ill 155
    As the youngest of four suckt her breast
What leave sucking infants! —the clock tung eleven
She wisht that the capons first signal was given
The master & man wisht em sens was in heaven
    New lies added dangers exprest 160

She dozd now & then on her chair she woud lye
& they found like the cat she coud doze wi one eye
Nigh as fourpence a groat is the watches coud spy
    The plot were a rougish conscern
& they wisperd of fire arms in each others ear 165
But wisperd as loud as the stranger shoud hear
& talkd of their guns as a store house it where
    As she all her perrils might learn

Then to see what she woud do they made a mock sleep
Dogs close to their master did watchfully keep 170
The woman play[d] chances & off did she creep
    As soft as she coud to the door
The way that she went'd made any one dread
She seemd as she wisht to have lightnd her tread
As one strimes & steps where sick folks lye a bed 175
    Her feet scarcly prest on the floor

Doubts now were all cleard — out of doors she had got
A shrill whistle blew — & the master he shot
& will like an arrow brusht up to the spot
    & agen turnd the key on their guest 180
"All keep out as is out" in triumph sed will
A groan murmurd help a weak call faint & chill
Foot steps trampld gently — agen all were still
    Save the dogs who woud not be at rest

The rout soon disturbd all the lodge of its rest 185
The wenches for saftey rund nearly undrest
& hodge sorely frightend wi what he had guest
    Bawld out to know what were amiss
& soon as he heard twas his prophesied trick
& the theif were locked out — then he took up his stick 190
& bragd wi the best hadnt skulls a bin thick
    They might a seen easy in this

The master calld silence to listen if aught
Still tokend near danger but they coud hear nought
Save hodge who heard groans now & then as he thought 195
    & his stick was prepard in his fist
Some proposd take the gun & go see if they coud
Execution if twas done or not be as twoud
But as now matters stood — hodge he votes for some good
    & they from his caution desist 200

First cock shouted morning aloud from his shed
& minded em all what the stranger had sed
& they deemd it rare luck as they didnt go bed
    To leave the guised rogue to her sen
The maids offerd prayers for thus being preservd 205
The master reflected how theyd a been servd
& hodge in a moment most dryly observd
    Theyd none a seen daylight agen

& oft they calld silence now & then the dogs growl
But nothing was heard save the woop of an owl 210
& winds in the chimney — the weather was foul
    That mournfully wisperd alarm
Hodge coudnt help hearing a whistle & groan
But night & its terrors thank god they were flown
The morning thro cracks of the window shuts shown 215
    & light woud soon free em of harm

The scales now was turnd & in triumph hodge sed
What scores of opinions he had in his head
Which fearing theyd laugh at him worse then they had
    He kept em all in to his sen 220
He knew very well that her bosom was flat
Coud mark on her chin hairs as black as his hat
Saw her pull down her bonnet to hide it & that
    & scarce coud help hinting agen

The woman too slung herself back in her chair 225
& hodge sed he vain gogged will to look there
Blue stockings she wore as to that he coud sware
    Which he neer saw on woman before
& once in her rocking she tosst up her feet
He thought he saw breeches but kept it discreet 230
& thought as none else saw — his fears might consiet
    So he woudnt pretend to no more

Hodge sed he thought much what he dare not express
Twas a good for nought rouge in disguisd womans dress
His wit pleasd the master who coudnt say less 235
    Then a worthy reward he shoud have
& all bragd of courage what each woud have done
How that woud a servd em how this wi his gun
Woud a rallied down two at a level like fun
    As all out of danger are brave 240

When darkness grew thin & the twilighty red
Like beauty thro veils began dimly to spread
They took up their weapons the stoutest hearts led
    & venturd to see what they coud
The door soon as opend the dogs rushed out 245
& tracked the causway & snufted about
& soon was the masters shot provd wi out doubt
    The dogs lap'd a puddle of blood

Good god they was sorry & felt for her pain
The groans which they heard this did quickly explain 250
& they called the dogs up to track her again
    To besure shed lye dead further on
They searched the yard under cribs did they peep
& rooted the straw where it seemd in a heap
As to dye out of sight any where she woud creep 255
    But the wounded encroacher was gone

Holes & corners they hunted for hours round & round
But nothing of rogues dead or living was found
Tho sure enough some one had got a deep wound
& the living helpd off wi the lame 260
The morn past opinions but nothing was heard
All day the[y] expected but nothing appeard
Hodge went to the village conjectures he heard
But nothing for truth never came

This friend & that wi opinions ran oer 265
Wi tidings of this that & tother hurt sore
They knew they was hurt but they knew nothing more
Suspicion might think as she woud
The farmer such stories did little regard
But trebld the strength of his guns & his yard 270
& thought to be stronger gen dangers prepard
Were the only best means for his good

& he thankd all his men for the courage theyd shewn
& he gen em that day from their labour a boon
& in reason what ale they likd drink morn & noon 275
Keeping guard for the nighttime in view
As to hodge for his service — the master declard
He merited honour as well as reward
& he placd him from thence the head boy in his yard
& a bran spanking whip gave him too 280

& still he continued to live at the lodge
& if by a woman rogue playd such a dodge
He vowd to remember the caution of hodge
& think em to trapping inclind
& when a chap lay awaken in bed 285
& heard the first crow of the cock from his shed
He thought what the woman drest robber had sed
& brought it all fresh in his mind

[The Two Soldiers]

I love to hear a summer tale
When all the fields are green
When sheep are grazing hill & dale
& villagers are seen
On sundays taking pleasant walks 5
Through corn & grass & hay
& maidens lost in laughing talk
Along their milking way

Oft bending by a stile to look
At wild flowers in the sun 10
Or leaning by a gravel brook
To see the waters run
Where wood bines arch & wilding rose
In leaning posture stands
They fearing oft to soil their cloaths 15
Sip water from their hands

When shepherds talk the sun to bed
By awthorn shaded brooks
In storys that were never read
In any printed books 20
& Goody who from maidenhood
Had traced the summer vales
No doubt had taste turned out as good
Knew many better tales

But darkness & the hasty rain 25
& noisy roaring wind
Brought like an ancient song again
The story to her mind

The night was dismal dark the rain
Fell with the falling leaves 30
& patted at the window pane
& rattled from the eaves
The cottage fire was blazing bright
The kitling full of mirth
Sat crouching in the corner light 35
For crickets on the [h]earth

& circling round a merry group
Sat listening to the rain
Till goody lapt her knitting up
To tell a tale again 40
She told about an ancient hall
That stood so very lone
She mentioned ivy on the wall
In terrors undertone

The very thought it checkt her breath 45
Lone midnight on the moores
For furze that blossom on the heath
Grew almost to the doors
& woods that tempests seldom miss
That raves & howls & roars 50
To scare on such a night as this
The gard dog out of doors

To say twas true she couldnt stop
But almost could declare
Whoso looked up the chimney top 55
Would see the branches there
The gentleman who owned the hall
On travel far away
Left servant folks in number small
To guard it night & day 60

The girls by custom like to men
Nigh overcome their fears
Till winds blew loud at night & then
They'd try to stop their ears
Though doors where safe & locks where strong 65
When watch dogs barked about
They dare not speak nor sing a song
But put the candles out

One dark & drear december night
One just got up to look 70
& lit another candle light
To fetch a pleasant book
For there was many books indeed
To sweeten solitude
& they would very often read 75
When in a reading mood

For all the neighbours dwelling near
Where those upon the shelves
The servant men in spite of fear
Oft left them to themselves 80
She stopt awhile the fire to stir
& put an apple down
To roast — & muttered as to her
She'd never leave a town

The maid just got into a chair 85
To look the volume oer
But ere she found a story there
A rap was at the door
She hurried out & dropt the light
Her heart was dropping too 90
Both in a corner crushed out right
& knew not what to do

A voice called out that they had lost
The way & meant no ill
& so the maidens hoped at most 95
For every dog was still
Two soldiers they had left the road
While crossing heath & more
& one had brothers gone abroad
So she unlocked the door 100

Now goody let the story stop
A minute in her mind
While louder in the chimney top
& louder got the wind
She said what many may have said 105
In such a night what joy
To have a house above their heads
To keep them warm & dry

The apples leisure to regale
Were roasted to the core 110
So from their patience & her tale
She stole a minute more
Soldiers though men of guns & swords
Know kindliness as well
& have a mort of tender words 115
That suit the women well

They pardon craved for knocking there
By travel sore distrest
The maids in pity set the chairs
An hour or two to rest 120
They talked so honest to the maids
Both hoped them honest men
Nay one was not a bit affraid
& felt no terror then

For she'd a brother far from home 125
That wouldn't hurt a flye
The other wished the dogs would come
To show a guard was nigh
She dare not let her courage fail
Or let them understand 130
Her fears so when her cheek turned pale
She leaned upon her hand

The soldiers talked of foreign parts
Till coming from without
A whistle made the maidens start 135
& then they heard a shout
Then somthing trampled near the place
& voices muttered near
They looked up in each others face
& dare not speak for fear 140

Then louder still as in the room
& horses on the moor
They heard & thought the master come
Yet terror barred the door
Twas well they did let who would come 145
The latch was gently tried
The maidens hallooed Tom the Groom
But ne'er a voice replied

Yet such a noise & such a shock
More loud then danger calls 150
Gave at the door a thundering knock
So loud it shook the walls
Who knocked one said & all looked up
In goodys face for dread
& had a owl began to whoop 155
They'd all been drove to bed

Who knocked that granny could not show
So fear out mastered mirth
The old man in the moon might know
But none could tell on earth 160
& many noises went & came
& both the soldiers then
Showed they were free from doubting blame
& down right honest men

They heard the maidens tales of doubt 165
& bade them both be still
& listened at the noise without
Yet feared for nothing ill
For they had met all sorts of fear
That like the clouds in may 170
Lost all their dread in coming near
& grew from black to grey

They h[e]ard but never cared to quake
& knew no reason why
Noises the winds could never make 175
Although the winds was high
& just to drive the noises back
That round the house begun
They reached it from the kitchen rack
& charged the rusty gun 180

Then gently threw the window up
To get the muzzle through
& kneeling heard another whoop
& then a whistle blew
They listened wether light or dark 185
If thieves were on the spot
They would be near enough the mark
To fright em so they shot

A sound as somthing shot again
A groan & somthing fell 190
But still they feared the cow was slain
What else they couldnt tell
& yet the noises came & went
& steps at every door
Traced round the house for some intent 195
They knew & nothing more

When morning did the sparrows send
To chelp the news of day
Twas like a letter from a friend
Or sweetheart far away 200
Glad as a present from abroad
From friendship that had crost
The sea in ships when all on board
In some old news was lost

The maids from windows round the hall 205
Looked out both far & near
The grape leaves shivered by the wall
As if they quaked for fear
But nothing could they hear or see
& yet so frit they was 210
They sturted backwards when the bee
Came buzz agen the glass

& soon as light gave leave to see
In garden ground & shed
The soldiers searched to ease & free 215
The maids of every dread
Yet in the gravel by the door
Fresh places might be seen
The foot marks plain where one or more
Had on some errand been 220

Where sluthering footsteps slipt aside
Ridged up the gravel lay
As some had struggled & had tried
To stand or get away
& there a spot of blood appeared 225
Where somthing seemed to fall
& sure enough twas known & feared
Thieves meant to rob the hall

The listeners round where glad at heart
& goody felt delight 230
That soldiers took the maidens part
& found the hall that night

But granny where was Tom the Groom
A little urchin said
Who chased the kitling round the room 235
With dancing cork & thread
That Goodys story couldnt show
But guessed he ran away
His sweetheart in the town below
Wept for him many a day 240

The soldiers they had met with scars
As soldiers mostly do
& they had been in morts of wars
Twas all that goody knew
But still the story went to say 245
(Maids should love honest men)
That though they forced to go away
They both returned agen

The Cross Roads or Haymakers Story

Stopt by the storm that long in sullen black
From the south west staind its encroaching track
Haymakers hussling from the rain to hide
Sought the grey willows by the pasture side
& there while big drops bow the grassy stems 5
& bleb the withering hay with pearly gems
Dimple the brook & patter in the leaves
The song & tale an hours restraint relieves
& while the old dames gossip at their ease
& pinch the snuff box empty by degrees 10
The young ones join in loves delightfull themes
Truths told by gipsys & expounded dreams
& mutterd things kept secrets from the rest
Of sweethearts names & who they love the best
& dazzling ribbons they delight to show 15
The last new favours of some weigling beau
That with such treacherey trys their hearts to move
& like the highest bribes the maidens love
The old dames jealous of their wisperd praise
Throw in their hints of mans deluding ways 20
& one to give her counsels more effect
& by examples illustrate the fact
Of innoscence oercome by flattering man
Thrice tappd her box & pinchd & thus began
"Now wenches listen & let lovers lye 25
"Yell hear a story ye may profit bye
"Im your age threble wi some oddments to't
"& right from wrong can tell if yell but do't
"Ye neednt giggle underneath yer hats
"Mines no joke matters let me tell you that 30
"So keep yer quiet till my storys told
"& dont despise yer betters cause theyre old
"I wish ye well upon my soul I do
"& just another pinch & Ill pursue
"That grave yeve heard off were the four roads meet 35
"Were walks the spirit in a winding sheet

"Oft seen at night by strangers passing late
"& tarrying neighbours that at market wait
"Stalking along as white as driven snow
"& s longs ones shadow when the sun is low 40
"The girl thats buried there I knew her well
"& her whol[e] history if yell hark can tell
"Her name was Jane & neighbours childern we
"& old companions once as ye may be
"& like to you on sundays often strolld 45
"To Gipseys camps to have our fortunes told
"& oft god rest her, in the fortune book
"Which we at hay time in our pockets took
"Our pins at blindfold on the wheel have stuck
"When hers woud always prick the worst of luck 50
"For try poor thing as often as she might
"Her point woud always on the blank alight
"Which plainly shows the fortune ones to have
"As such like go unwedded to the grave
"& so it provd — the next succeeding may 55
"We both went service from our sports & play
"Tho in the village still as friends & kin
"Thought neighbours service better to begin
"As they considerd planning for the best
"Theyd be more kind then strangers woud at first 60
"So out we went Janes place was reckond good
"Tho she 'bout life but little understood
"For she'd a master wild as wild can be
"& far unfit for such a child as she
"& soon the wisper went about the town 65
"That Janes good looks procurd her many a gown
"From him whose promise was to every one
"But whose intention was to wive with none
"Twas nought to wonder tho begun by guess
"For Jane was lovly in her sunday dress 70
"& all expected such a rosey face
"Woud be her ruin — as was just the case
"The while the change was easily percievd
"Some months went by ere I such tales believd

"For theres such people nowadays Lord knows 75
"Woud sooner hatch up lies then mend their cloahs
"& when wi such like tattle they begin
"Dont mind whose character they spoil a pin
"Else passing neighbours often markd em smile
"& watchd him take her milkpail oer a stile 80
"& many a time as wandering closer bye
"From Jenneys bosom met an heavy sigh
"& often markd her as discoursing deep
"As doubts might rise to give just cause to weep
"In smoth[er]ing notice by a wisht disguise 85
"To slive her apron corner to her eyes
"Such signs were mournfull & alarming things
"& far more weighty then conjecture brings
"Tho foes made double what they heard of all
"Swore lies as proofs & prophysied her fall 90
"Poor thoughtless wench it seems but sunday past
"Sin we went out together for the last
"& plain enough indeed it was to find
"Shed somthing more then common on her mind
"For she was always fond & full of chat 95
"In passing harmless jokes 'bout beaus & that
"But nothing then was scarcly talkd about
"& what there was I even forcd it out
"A gloomy wanness spoilt her rosey cheek
"& doubts hung there that was not mine to seek 100
"She neer so much as mentiond things to come
"But sighd oer pleasures ere she left her home
"& now & then a mournfull smile woud raise
"At freaks repeated of our younger days
"As I brought up while passing spots of ground 105
"Where we when childern hurly burly'd round
"Or blind mans bluffd some morts of hours away
"Two games poor thing Jane dearly lovd to play
"She smild at these but shook her head & sighd
"When ere she thought my look was turnd aside 110
"Nor turnd she round as was her former way
"To praise the thorn white over then with may

"Nor stooped once tho thousands round her grew
"To pull a cowslip as she usd to do
"For Jane in flowers delighted from a child 115
"I like the garden but she lovd the wild
"& oft on sundays young mens gifts declind
"Poesys from gardens of the sweetest kind
"& eager scrambd the single rose to get
"& woodbine flowers at every bush she met 120
"& cowslip blossom with its ruddy streak
"Woud tempt her furlongs from the pad to seek
"& gay long purple with its tufty spike
"Shed wade oer shoes to reach it in the dyke
"& oft while scratting thro the briery woods 125
"For tempting cuckoo flowers & vi'let buds
"Poor Jane Ive known her crying sneak to town
"& fear her mother when shed tore her gown
"Ah these were days her conscience viewd wi pain
"Which all are loath to loose as well as Jane 130
"& what I took more odd then all the rest
"Was that same night she neer a wish exprest
"To see the gipseys so belovd before
"That lay a stones throw from us on the moor
"I hinted it she just replyd agen 135
"She once believd 'em but had doubts since then
"& when we sought our cows I calld 'cum mull'
"But she stood silent for her heart was full
"She lovd dumb things & ere she milkd begun
"To fuss & stroke them more then ere shed done 140
"& tho her tears stood watering in her eye
"I little took it as her last good bye
"For she was tender & Ive often known
"Her mourn for beetles thats bin trampld on
"So I neer dreamd from this what soon befell 145
"Till the next morning rung her passing bell
"My storys long but times in plenty yet
"Sin the black clouds betoken nought but wet
"& Ill een snatch a minutes breath or two
"& take another pinch to help me thro 150

"So as I sed next morn I heard the bell
"& passing neighbours crossd the street to tell
"That my poor partner Jinney had been found
"In the old flag pool on the pasture drownd
"God knows my heart I twitterd like a leaf 155
"& found too late the cause of sundays grief
"For every tongue was loosd to gabble oer
"The slanderous things that secrets passd before
"Wi truth or lies they neednt then be strickt
"The one they raild at coudnt contradict 160
"Twas now no secret of her being beguild
"& every mouth knew Jinny dyd wi child
"& tho more cautious with a living name
"They more then guessd her master bore the blame
"That very morning it affects me still 165
"Ye know the foot pad sidles down the hill
"Ign'rant as babe unborn I passd the pond
"To milk as usual in our close beyond
"& cows were drinking at the waters edge
"& horses brousd among the flags & sedge 170
"& nats & migens dancd the water oer
"Just as Ive markd em scores o' times before
"& birds sat singing as in mornings gone
"While I as unconsernd went soodling on
"But little dreaming as the wakening wind 175
"Flappd the broad ash leaves oer the pond reclind
"& oer the water crinkd the curdld wave
"That Jane was sleeping in her watery grave
"The netterd boy that usd to tend the cows
"While getting whip sticks from the dangling boughs 180
"Of osiers drooping by the water side
"Her bonnet floating on the top espyd
"He knew it well & hastnd fearful down
"To take the terror of his fears to town
"A melancholly story far too true 185
"& soon the village to the pasture flew
"Were from the deepest hole the pond about
"They draggd poor Jinneys lifless body out

"& took her home were scarce an hour gone bye
"She had bin living like to you & I 190
"I went wi more & kissd her for the last
"& thought wi tears on pleasures that were past
"& the last kindness left me then to do
"I went at milking were her blossoms grew
"& handfulls got of rose & lambtoe sweet 195
"& put them with her in her winding sheet
"A wilfull murder jury made the crime
"Nor parson 'lowd to pray nor bell to chyme
"On the cross roads far from her friends & kin
"The usual law for such ungodly sin 200
"Who violent hands upon themselves have laid
"Poor Janes last bed unchristian like was made
"& there like all whose last thoughts turn to heaven
"She sleeps & doubtless hopd to be forgiven
"& tho I sayt for maids thus weigld in 205
"I think the wicked men deserve the sin
"& sure enough we all at last shall see
"The treachery punishd as it ought to be
"For ere his wickedness pretended love
"Jane was Ill bound as spotless as the dove 210
"&s good a servant still old folks alow
"As ever scourd a pail or milkd a cow
"& ere he led her into ruins way
"As gay & buxom as a summers day
"The birds that ranted in the hedgerow boughs 215
"As night & morning we have sought our cows
"With yokes & buckets as she bouncd along
"Were often deafd to silence with her song
"But now shes gone — girls shun decietfull men
"The worst of stumbles ye can fall agen 220
"Be deaf to them & then ast were yell see
"Yer pleasures safe as under lock & key
"Throw not my words away as many do
"Theyre gold in value tho theyre cheap to you
"& husseys hearken & be warnd from this 225
"If ye love mothers never do amiss

"Jane might love hers but she forsook the plan
"To make her happy when she thought of man
"Poor tottering dame it was too plainly known
"Her daughters dying hastend on her own 230
"For from the day the tydings reachd her door
"She took to bed & looked up no more
"& ere agen another year came round
"She well as Jane was laid within the ground
"& all was grievd poor goodys end to see 235
"No better neighbour enterd house then she
"A harmless body wi no 'busive tongue
"Trig as new pins & tights the day were long
"& go the week about nine times in ten
"Yed find her house as cleanly as her sen 240
"But Lord protect us time such change does bring
"We cannot dream what oer our heads may hing
"The very house she livd in stick & stone
"Sin goody dyd has tumbld down & gone
"& where the majoram ance & sage & rue 245
"& balm & mint wi curld leaf parsley grew
"& double marygolds & silver thyme
"& pumkins neath the window usd to climb
"& where I often when a child for hours
"Tryd thro the pails to get the tempting flowers 250
"As Ladys Laces everlasting peas
"True love lies bleeding with the hearts at ease
"& golden rods & tanzey running high
"That oer the pail tops smild on passers bye
"Flowers in my time that every one woud praise 255
"Tho thrown like weeds from gardens now adays
"Were these all grew now henbane stinks & spreads
"& docks & fissles shake their seedy heads
"& yearly keeps wi nettles smothering oer
"Nor house nor dame nor gardens known no more 260
"While neighbouring nigh one lonly eldern tree
"Is all thats left of what had us'd to be
"Marking the place & bringing up wi tears
"The recollections of ones younger years

"& now Ive done yere each at once as free 265
"To take yer trundle as ye usd to be
"To take right ways as Jinney shoud have taen
"Or headlong run & be a second Jane
"For by one thoughtless girl thats acted ill
"A thousand may be guided if they will 270
"As oft mong folks to labour bustling on
"We mark the foremost kick agen a stone
"Or stumble oer a stile they meant to climb
"While hind ones see & shun the fall in time
"But ye Ill bound fort like a mort the best 275
"Loves tickling nick nacks & the laughing jest
"& ten times sooner then be warnd by me
"Woud each be sitting on some fellows knee
"& sooner 'lieve the lyes wild chaps will tell
"Then old dames cautions who woud wish ye well 280
"So have yer wills" — she pinchd her box again
& ceasd her tale & listnd to the rain
Which still as usual patterd fast around
& bowd the bent head loaded to the ground
While larks their naked nests by force forsook 285
Prund their wet wings in bushes by the brook
The maids impatient now old goody ceasd
As restless childern from the school releasd
Right gladly proving what she'd just foretold
That young ones stories was preferd to old 290
Turn to the wisperings of their former joy
That oft decieve but very rarely cloy

The Memory of Love

A Tale

Once in the merry toil of clipping time
When suns are hot & summers in her prime
An old man laboring with his fellow men
Neath two broad wallnuts shadowing oer the pen
To lighten labour & make short the day 5
They tund old songs & chatterd time away
Some bragging oer the feats of younger years
Of quickness some to use the snipping sheers
Others of strength & agilty the while
When they coud leap a ditch or jump a stile 10
One told the history of his dog with pride
That half asleep lay panting by his side
The young ones harpd of coming holidays
& pretty maids & dances had their praise
Of those they sought & fools that had believd 15
& dreamd of marriage till they woke decievd
Twas thought no sin if hearts they only won
To make them ach they thought it precious fun
Old robin heard em tween a sigh & smile
& bade them listen to his tale awhile 20
They stopt & choakd the titter as he spoke
& heard his story as one hears a joke
Thinking him childish as his mind woud cling
Wi joy to such a silly seeming thing
The vulgar dregs of love was all they knew 25
But what hed felt was tender puer & true
"My boys" says he "I once was young & wild
"Urging my follys when a maiden smild
"Oft whispering marriage wi a foolish tongue
"& then excusd me as some years too young 30
"I courted beauty till the freak was past
"& then found others prettier then the last
"I wood & won them as a sort of pride

"& then sought others till I was denied
"Nor coud their sighs affect my roving will 35
"I left them off in search of prettier still
"Laugh not my boys when slighted maidens mourn
"For fear your follys may be servd in turn
"& if in beautys net ye once shoud be
"Yell find a puzzle ere your hearts are free 40
"I left my old place wi the finishd year
"& went to service in a village near
"Stretchd from the last but some few country miles
"In crooked pathways over dykes & styles
"Were foolish freaks my fancys did renew 45
"& folly sweetend as each face was new
"But there one beauty met my wandering eye
"& bound my fancys wi a troubld tye
"I tryd to break it but it woud not bend
"So freaks & lyes & follys had their end 50
"Her very image startles on me yet
"She seemd the lovliest I had ever met
"Her face chilld thro me tho twas only fair
"& red & rosey as a manys are
"& tho her bosom swelld & eyes shone bright 55
"As others shine they overpowerd me quite
"In every feature shone that witching spell
"That love adores & language cannot tell
"To my new place I went at michaelmass
"When roads were splashy but green leaves & grass 60
"Brought this sweet blossom wi the early may
"To win the wandering of my heart away
"Hird at a mayday statute & her name
"Was talk about the village ere she came
"Maids jealous whisperings did their doubtings raise 65
"While chaps was eager tho by guess to praise
"& I who meant a seasons suit to prove
"Met wi a fruitless & a lasting love
"The day she came I reccolect it still
"As wi a cart I journeyd to the mill 70

"She passd me by her face I cant forget
"The sweetest may flower I had ever met
"The morn was lovly & down lane & balk
"I went in joy & musd along the walk
"Gazing on prospects in a happy vein 75
"Oer fields fresh ploughd & springing crops of grain
"& all I met & all that pleasd my eye
"Time neer had power to push their memory bye
"I still remember how each close was lind
"Wi cowslip bunches nodding in the wind 80
"& in each lane oer hung wi briar & thorn
"What swarms of daiseys glitterd in the morn
"My dog was happy too & often rolld
"His curly jacket in the fresh ploughd mold
"& sheep that woud my dog a moment heed 85
"Rose from their lares & stoopd adown to feed
"The hare oft sturted from the clover lea
"& birds were happy as a song can be
"The red caps often from the hedge woud drop
"& whistling perch upon the thistle top 90
"The weeders toild & sung their hours away
"& while the old ones askd the time of day
"The young girls hallood merrily & shill
"If I woud take a partner to the mill
"Nor did I think a heart as glad as theirs 95
"Woud meet a cause to change my joy to cares
"The roaring mill brook whose uneven tide
"Grows now & then more then a horse can stride
"Till from the mill releasd its windings creep
"Narrow & soft a green grass hoppers leap 100
"She passd me there I turnd an anxious eye
"& had one askd I coud not answer why
"Twas her I thought that wore the village fame
"& ere I judg'd it provd the very same
"She askd the way & wi a timid smile 105
"Turnd back to thank me ere she skipt the stile
"I wishd Id offerd help when she was bye

"To cross the brook but it was nearly dry
"Nor on the bank she sighd to be alone
"Nor pausd before she stept from stone to stone 110
"Filld full of fancys to my journeys end
"I wishd Id spoke then judgd I might offend
"Then wishd the brook its stones had over run
"& stretchd a danger which she coud not shun
"Without my help that I by chance might prove 115
"A feeble shadow of my sudden love
"Within the foldings of her ankerchief
"Was pind a red pink wi its crimson leaf
"The little trifle gave my bosom pain
"I thought it given by some parting swain 120
"& ever since my memory keeps awake
"To love the blossom for the owners sake
"& every year as clipping time comes round
"When ere I see one in our poseys bound
"Tho I am old & love has lost its power 125
"I pause & sigh & een coud kiss the flower
"& think the maiden be she plain or fair
"Like her I lovd because she placd it there
"I often went on sundays to the spot
"Were she passd by a trifle neer forgot 130
"The very stones she stept to cross the stream
"Ive sat for hours to muse upon & dream
"The stile too over which I saw her climb
"Has made my foolish heart ach many a time
"& tho Im old my palsid memory still 135
"If I passd now woud turn my bosom chill
"On the next morning as I crossd the plain
"At milkings hour I saw the maid again
"The cows stood round her in a wondering way
"& being a stranger kept her fears at bay 140
"They tossd their heads & snufft the morning gales
"& skewd at her — I gladly took the pails
"& tho my sheep that almost seemd to scold
"Me when I went was noising in the fold

"I milkd em all & more her fears to screen 145
"I took her yokes & saw her oer the green
"& at the pasture gate wi fond delight
"I left a promise I woud milk at night
"& urgd her kind return that shed agree
"My may game partner at the eve to be 150
"She lookd consent I even thought she smild
"For love sees double when by hope beguild
"But as the cows grew reconsild & tame
"She always thankd me but refusd the claim
"To milk or bear it home from evens toil 155
"& een refusd assistance oer a stile
"It made me half my hopful love resign
"& feel her heart had but small room for mine
"Yet I urgd on & woud my doubts reprove
"& often thought she desbeleevd my love 160
"I went to church each leisure sabbath day
"For every purpose but the right to pray
"Her seat was opposite to mine — in vain
"I tryd to read & turnd to gaze again
"Till some old woman shook her serious head 165
"& urgd my eye to what I seldom read
"My book was open oft when prayers were done
"& Ive kept reading till the psalms begun
"When the clerks voice & basoon booming deep
"Made memory startle as Id been asleep 170
"I often tryd what signals love woud take
"But she seemd strange to all I had to make
"I often smild when ere she turnd her eye
"But she woud pause as if she wonderd why
"She seemd to try to shun me in the street 175
"& I scarce consious tryd the maid to meet
"At length some gipseys on our comon came
"& as a change to may nights even game
"Maids in the gipseys nook proposd a dance
"& I went too & dreamd upon the chance 180
"For summer eves to servants then supplyd

"Sweet leisure hours when toil was thrown aside
"Masters & misses too woud join the play
"& ramp as equals in the sports of may
"In my young days soon as the ruddy sun 185
"Was set our labour in the fields was done
"& we have playd & dancd when day was bye
"Till the moons horns crept half way up the sky
"Young miss & master servant man & maid
"& none woud scold nor question why we staid 190
"The maiden came her whom I wished to see
"I askd her trembling if shed dance with me
"She smild then checkt it & wi half turnd eye
"Pausd for a moment ere she made reply
"Good manners seemd to urge her to consent 195
"She blushd & yielded & away we went
"O the first time I touchd her gentle hand
"I felt a joy yell never understand
"Unless ye chill neath true loves extacy
"& then yell own the pleasant pain wi me 200
"My heart sunk in me like a lump of clay
"My feet een trembld as we dancd away
"& then the trembling left me & in turn
"Hot feverish flushes made it seem to burn
"I viewd her face were beauty near coud cloy 205
"& dreamd oer raptures till I smild for joy
"Some sneerd contempt & whisperingly abusd
"& others turnd away & seemd confusd
"To see me chuse a stranger from the throng
"& shun the partners I had known so long 210
"I prest her hand she turnd a tender eye
"But never smild & often seemd to sigh
"& when a finish to the sports had come
"I offerd hints to see her safly home
"She turnd aside & never answerd no 215
"But thankd me kindly & prepard to go
"& warm wi raptures dreams in hopes delay
"I led her homward on our evening way

"& venturd gradual hints & smiles & sighs
"To clear my passion of its thin disguise 220
"She seemd confusd at what she had to say
"Nor bade hopes live nor wishd my words away
"At length she tryd & when she choakd the sigh
"She gave me hints that made them hurry bye
" 'Nay you may love' she said '& Id believe 225
"If I had power but why shoud I decieve'
"Then pausd as loath the finish to relate
"& woud have left me but I held the gate
"She sighd to see me toy wi hopes & fears
"& made excuses to conseal her tears 230
"Wiping her dark brown curls from either eye
"As shrinking from me she exclaimd 'good bye'
"& bade me cease to say she had my heart
"& struggld from me as resolvd to part
" 'Your hearts not mine' she said '& I must shun 235
"Your urgd returns for mines already won
"What ever proofs your vows or words make known
"I cannot give you what is not my own'
"Then loosd the gate & hurried to the door
"& I beheld her wi hopes eyes no more 240
"For often to the town her lover came
"& came at last the marriage day to name
"I went to church not knowing what I did
"That very sunday when the bands was bid
"Lord help ones cares Id need enough to stay 245
"& think while there of better things & pray
"But when the parson brought the thing about
"I shut my book & sighd & venturd out
"& went I know not how nor were nor when
"But hopes wore off & I got better then 250
"The marriage came it was a woful day
"& memory gave it an eternal stay
"I heard the bells ring as I crossd the moor
"& never heard so sad a peal before
"I wishd to see how she woud look a bride 255

"& started off & then my courage dyd
"I woud not go & then I venturd bye
"The church yard wall but nothing met my eye
"I felt as happy that the thing was oer
"& then as vexd I did not go before 260
"I hung my head half shamd along the street
"Nor card to talk wi those my path woud meet
"Lest they shoud jeer me or bring up the day
"So when they spoke I mumbling sneakd away
"I thought upon her lovly face for years 265
"Wi fondest feelings almost kin to tears
"Till the heart achd wi love—I cannot tell
"What others thought by her I lovd so well
"Or how she seemd to him that calld her wife
"Her face to me was memory for life 270
"Her looks her ways in winning forms woud steal
"& left a pain I never ceasd to feel
"Her very voice woud memorys partner be
"& music lingerd in the sound wi me
"Her troubling form was long about my sight 275
"Oer day dreams dozing or in sleep by night
"My dreams wore constantly that pleasing pain
"The face of her I lovd & coud not gain
"& oft I see that moving scene renewd
"& as she passd I seemingly pursued 280
"Somtimes in vain & oft as wide awake
"I saw her stop & smile at my mistake
"Changd to a face I never saw before
"& all my shadows of delight was oer
"& wishd that pleasure vainly een in sleep 285
"Were fancy pictures its delusions deep
"I wishd when waking I coud feel the bliss
"& venturd one imaginary kiss
"That seeming pleasure might to memory cling
"But even this my dreams woud never bring 290
"I sought at first the noise of feast & fair
"To see if tumult yet had joys to spare

"& hopes woud somtimes join my pleasant way
"Thro fields & meads in summer cloathing gay
"Half sad half pleasd I musd oer what might come 295
"& idly brushd the meadow flowers in bloom
"& when I saunterd mid the noisey fair
"Memory woud taunt me who was wanted there
"& oft I strove wi foolish search to find
"Some face like hers that I might change my mind 300
"I left on this & that an earnest eye
"& made some turn — no doubt to wonder why
"But all were blanks & made my wishes vain
"& search for cure still added all to pain
"The showmans shouts which wonder yearly brings 305
"The huge hung pictures of outlandish things
"Were grinning tigers waverd in the wind
"& raisd more wonders then was hid behind
"The merry fool that woud his speeches make
"Till wi the fun my very sides woud ach 310
"The turning organ & the jarring din
"Of shouts & music tempting gazers in
"Till crowds woud crush around the tempting shows
"& I crushd too nor card for trampld toes
"The jew cheats veigling voice 'who bys who bys' 315
"Wi white washd watches of inspiring size
"The rolling drum & soldiers gay cockade
"& fond encroachments of some simpering maid
"Pulling my sleeve & urging whispers low
"Memory of farings promisd long ago 320
"These all unnoticd now I saunterd bye
"& only turnd a carless ear or eye
"Seeking for that which it was vain to find
"To loose the burden from a troubld mind
"The dance & revel brought its joys no more 325
"I hated pastimes which I lovd before
"The walks on sabbath days wi milking lass
"& every pastime on the summer grass
"Were hunt the slipper passd the hours away

"& blindmens buff made every bosom gay 330
"When tittering maidens urgd me which to seize
"These lost the relish & the power to please
"& may day revels ownd their powers no more
"I sought no may bush for a lovers door
"Nor snatchd short sleeps to watch the morn begin 335
"To take her cows the garlands claims to win
"I saw none now that claimd an hour from sleep
"Nor none to care for but my dog & sheep
"I kept no 'may balls' now of cowslips made
"To toss on maydays to a favourd maid 340
"I ran no 'crookhorn' on the pasture grasses
"Nor 'duck neath water' playd wi bawling lasses
"Nor dancd the 'Maze' which shepherds fond of play
"Cut in the grass to baffle maids at may
"The self same puzzle which the knowing boy 345
"Oft draws at school & calls 'the road to troy'
"Nor 'lost love letter' round the whispering ring
"Coud one fe[i]nt pleasure to my musings bring
"My fancys found none in the merry game
"As worth the kisses which the finders claim 350
"I shund them all the sports & loves & ways
"That usd to please me in my hopfull days
"My sundays harmless pleasures were forsook
"Nor turnd my rambles to the pasture brook
"Were in my youth at 'Eastwells' fountain side 355
"Which winters never froze nor summer dryd
"Young men & maidens usd to talk & play
"In the cool shadows of its willows grey
"Drinking loves healths in totts of sugard drink
"On the soft swellings of its rushy brink 360
"From the spring head like winter cold & chill
"Were boils the white sand that is never still
"Now swimming up in silver threads & then
"Slow siling down to bubble up agen
"There shepherds usd to sit & tell the while 365
"Their tales & jokes to win each maidens smile

"& drank loud flattering healths to those they lovd
"& turnd to pause & see if they approvd
"The maids lookd down & blushd till none percievd
"Then smild a token which their hearts believd 370
"I shund all these which I had lovd before
"& joind the childens play games on the moor
"Nicking the 'nine peg morris' in the grass
"Or tying garlands for some little lass
"Reaching them roses from the hedgrow bowers 375
"Who fawnd around me till I got the flowers
"& turnd my labours to their changing wills
"Now willow whistles made then water mills
"Then plaited rush caps till they cloyd agen
"& fresh inventions were demanded then 380
"Midsummer cushions oft their taste woud court
"& mid the green corn off they chasd in sport
"& thus I tryd to loiter time away
"Till they were weary of each idle play
"I was the play king of the jocund clan 385
"& often wishd I coud forget the man
"That had but trifles happiness to spoil
"Play all their love & all their trouble toil
"Somtimes wi stretching hand they bent to look
"Flat stones & pebbles in the tinkling brook 390
"Making me jelt them oer the pond to make
"The bouncing jumps they title 'duck & drake'
"& mong the shutting daiseys on its banks
"As they grew sick & weary of their pranks
"Ive dropt adown at ruddy eventide 395
"& sat to hear them wonder at my side
"To see the water imitate the sky
"& the round moon miles thro the bottom lye
"Were the cloud man true to his evening place
"Stood in its light & lookd us in the face 400
"As tho he heard their merry shout & laugh
"Leaning like talking shepherd oer his staff
"Or weary woodman (& as such they guest

"The shade to be) bent oer his load to rest
"My partners as they passd woud point & say 405
"Theres love sick robin wi the boys at play
"Maidens woud think me justly servd & smild
"To see crossd love had made me twice a child
"Folks thought me crazd & you may think the same
"Who know of love no further then the name 410
"Think as ye please my childish tale is done
"Tis time it were for theres the setting sun
"& if ye ere shoud meet wi my despair
"To love a girl that has no love to spare
"Then will your weakness to their beauty bow 415
"& feel the truth that I have told you now"

Jockey & Jinney or First Love

A Tale

"Thoughtless of beauty she was beautys self"
Thomson [*The Seasons,* Autumn l.207]

Wereover many a stile neeth willows grey
The winding footpath leaves the public way
Free from the dusty din & ceasless chime
Of bustling waggons in the summer time
Crossing a brook — were braving storms in vain 5
Two willows fell & still for brigs remain
Corn field & clover closes leading down
In peacful windings to the neighbouring town
Were on bridge wall or rail or trees smooth bark
The passing eye is often stopt to mark 10
The artless vanity of village swains
Who spend a leisure hour with patient pains
& put to sculptors purposes the knife
To spin a cobweb for an after life
Nicking the letters of their little names 15
In rudest forms that untaught science frames
Pleasd with the feeblest shadow of renown
That warms alike the noble and the clown
Nigh to that path a sheltering hedge beside
A Cottage stands in solitary pride 20
Whose thatch with housleek flowers is yellowd oer
Where flock the bees from hives agen the door
Lonly & sweet as ever welcome spring
Neer fails its pleasant visitors to bring
Trees sheltering round it hide returning rooks 25
& twittering swallows seek its chimney nooks
In peace the sparrow chirps its joyous calls
& takes the feather to the crevisd walls
Nor fails the harmless robin & the wren
To seek such sweet secluded haunts agen 30
Beneath the eaves the martins still repair
& yearly build their mortard dwelling there

Here Jinney livd to grace the lovly scenes
Fair as the spring sweet blushing in her teens
& mid her flowers & linnets wistling nigh 35
Has often met the strangers passing eye
Beneath the eldern sitting in the cool
Knitting her hoes or winding at her spool
The fairest village maid around for miles
Mingling by turns her dittys & her smiles 40
Her parents joy she was their hearts to glad
Their only hopes for she was all they had
Nor once their warmest wishes she decievd
She heard their counsels & their truth believd
With their advice thro life she journeyd on 45
Nor did a wrong unless to love be one
Tho in an humble way her friends livd well
& had their butter & their eggs to sell
While such like errands fell to Jinneys share
Who weekly went to market with her ware 50
Gracfully drest some lovers eye to win
For Jinneys bosom felt that harmless sin
Nor faild she long tho little done by dress
To crown her artless wishes with success
Once journ[ey]ing thither Jockey met her view 55
Opening the gate as she was passing thro'
She blushd supprise he bended oer his hook
& as she left him turnd him round to look
Her cheek was rosey for the day was warm
Her hat untyd & basket on her arm 60
She felt his look but never turnd agen
Shed long been cautiond not to stare at men
& as her hand that held with jealous trust
Her folded gown from sweeping in the dust
Let go with modest fears its hold behind 65
He felt more touchd & blest her in his mind
& tho she nimbly glided from his sight
Her face & manners left a fixt delight
& in his bosom found a lasting place
Time nor fresh faces coud no more deface 70

& Jinney felt she knew not hardly how
A fluttering somthing never known till now
She wonderd what the strangers look coud mean
& thought she likd him best of all shed seen
Nor coud she help conjecturing on the sight 75
& guessd & guess'd & hopd she guessd the right
Shed feign made light of all she thought she knew
But thoughts grew stronger as they older grew
Nor helpd she wishing in her reasons spite
Hed gen be there returning home at night 80
& spite of what her mother said of men
Hopd as she passd hed hold the gate agen
Meanwhile the swain with mellancholly speed
Pursued his toils & drove his flocks to feed
Go were he woud his mind was hard to please 85
His heart was wandering & but ill at ease
The hat untyd the rosey burning cheek
Was with him all the day & all the week
Nor woud they leave him while the night sojournd
In dreams the teazing pleasures still returnd 90
Jenny the same was often wakd from sleep
Wi clapping gates & bleat of droving sheep
& startling shepherds every now & then
Crossing her path & holding gates agen
Each market morning as she passd the place 95
Past reccolections reddend in her face
The strangers look rose burning in her mind
& made her often turn to look behind
While virgin fears in matters yet untryd
Woud feign forget it but the heart denyd 100
As when in dreams the stranger shepherd came
She seemd to flye & hide her head for shame
But soon as woke — the startling vision bye
To find 'em dreams she coudnt help but sigh
Thus weeks & months wi' Jocky & wi Jane 105
Finishd their rounds & toild em oer again
Finding each heart in blindfold hopes the same
& leaving heavier every time they came

Each felt & wishd what neither dard pursue
& each as warmly lovd but neither knew 110
Jockey had known her name ere sin the day
He met the maiden on her market way
Ere sin he op'd the gate in hopes to please
& for his kindness lost his heart & ease
By passing folks then made enqu[i]reys good 115
Of whom she was & were her cottage stood
& oft essayd to start when doubts delayd
& spoilt but every resolution made
As reason turnd him round to think awhile
Dropt on a hill or leaning oer a stile 120
Judging how vain such follys to pursue
To be a fool & thus declare it too
By seeking one he never knew before
& ask admission at a strangers door
Where jealous dames or grannys might reside 125
& take his visit on the blackest side
To think him one who came with vile excuse
Their artless Jinneys ignorance to seduce
For such are often by experience wise
& knows seduction masks in loves disguise 130
& most old women have a jealous fear
That doubts of tokens speaking most sincere
Deeming the ways that wooers have to win
A dangerous poison in a gilden skin
& lovers oft from their suspecting doubt 135
Have mountains as it were to climb about
& ere they gain their wishes meet from hence
The worst of pains attendant on suspence
Thus Jockey thought as onward he sojournd
& started often & as oft returnd 140
He doubted much & dreaded to attend
Loves fickle footsteps to its journeys end
Till on a sunday fully bent he rose
To mend or bring the matter to a close
& thus attird in his best hopes & dress 145
His heart warmd often thinking on success

Then dampt again but wether fail or speed
He journeyd on determind to proceed
Soon Jennys cottage rose upon his sight
Enquirey questiond & it was the right 150
A boy was tending horses near the spot
Who showd the pathway leading to the cott
& answering things which Jockey lovd to hear
Reviving hopes & lessening many a fear
As how the friends of Jinney were as free 155
As any people living need to be
& as for her shed every bodys praise
For modest manners & good naturd ways
& as thus far when Jockey matters found
& to the point contrivd to veigle round 160
Bout who kept Jinney company & that
The boy guessd matters cockd his napless hat
Rose up & gan his horses names to bawl
& leeving turnd to mumble "none at all"
Twas quite enough just as he wishd forsooth 165
Far as boys storys might be taen for truth
It lightnd up his heart such things to find
& made him hope success was in the wind
The cottage door was now upon his view
The twisting woodbines round the window grew 170
The birds were wistling—ah how blest they seemd
To be so near the object he esteemd
An odd cow fed upon the neighbouring moor
& three cade lambs were playing near the door
Who livd by tender care & tamely stood 175
To sip from Jennys hand their daily food
Now past remembrance gan to flutter high
To think the lovly stranger was so nigh
& former doubts rose topmost in their sway
& hopes on point to blossom dyd away 180
To see her gen hed just go wander round
& end the rest when better chance was found
The dog gun barking as he crossd the moor
The poultry noisd & open came the door

Trifles een scares in such a lonly place 185
Were even birds dislike a strangers face
Jockey just turnd a shanny sideling eye
To see who noticd as he lingerd bye
Ah now thy courage love — twas past with him
A shivering ague trembld every limb 190
His hearts sensations oer its past delight
Een flutterd like a birds as well it might
That self same look that beautys lingering beams
Kept bright so long by fancy & by dreams
That very face which he one morning met 195
& thought it lovliest he'd ere seen as yet
For whom the gate was opd & shut wi sighs
That lovley girl was now before his eyes
What must he say fear fixt him to the spot
He woud have made excuse but had it not 200
Love is so timid while it is so young
He coud not own it how his heart was wrung
Yet inly wishd the while that she but knew
What he coud tell so tender & so true
His looks had meaning but young loves are shy 205
& plainest questions promt a first reply
But false hopes pleasant while the test is tryd
He durst not speak for fear of being denyd
Tho Jinnys sweet simplicity & grace
Denyd ill nature in her lovley face 210
& half confirmd it as he shoold along
By saying "good day" but Jockeys skill was young
He knew it not or dare not yet pursue
The little chances which in love he knew
His hearts flushd wish the faultering tongue denyd 215
He turnd to speak but only lookd & sighd
& as he twirld his stick & soodld on
He left his blessing were his heart was gone
For such good nature at a strangers door
Made love burn stronger then it did before 220
& from that hour he vowd none else shoud be
His future wife if Jinny woud agree

There lay the doubt which paind his heart to think
Nor let him nightly hardly sleep a wink
& thus in anguish as he homward went 225
Oer gate & stile conjecturingly he bent
Making resolves as soon as he coud find
A chance renewd to boldly speak his mind
& deep repenting over what was past
To be so foolish as let slip the last 230
Great was the conflict labouring in his breast
Which only lovers can explain the best
Conscerns of love are dangerously deferd
Ere equal oppertunitys occurd
A bolder lover might drop in the while 235
& all the present hopes entirely spoil
He knew it well & dreaded what he knew
A maid so blooming & so lovley too
Like blossoms blooming fairer then the rest
Attention drew from every one that past 240
Urgd every eye with tempting gaze to turn
& left some hearts with quicker pulse to burn
In sleepless pain that night was passd away
His heart had left him & his thoughts astray
Fancy was picturing in his wandering head 245
How Jane was sleeping in her peacfull bed
Unconsious there of all he felt & knew
Of how he lovd & dreaded to pursue
& tossd & turnd while coward consience chid
To meet such chance & pass it as he did 250
But all was vain the past was past as then
& too far travelld to be calld agen
Yet ere he turnd him to retreating rest
These wilder wishes left his aching breast
"Ah powerfull night was but thy chances mine 255
Had I but ways to come at joys as thine
Spite of thy wizard look & sable skin
The ready road to bliss tis thine to win
All nature owns of beautiful or sweet
In thy embraces now unconsious meet 260

Young Jinney ripening into womanhood
That hides from day like lilys while in bud
To thy grim visage blooms in all her charms
& comes like eve unblushing to thy arms
Of thy black mantle coud I be possest 265
How woud I pillow on her panting breast
& try those lips were trial rude beseems
& breath my spirit in her very dreams
That neer a thought might wander from her heart
But I possest it or ensurd a part 270
Of all the blessing[s] that belong to thee
Had I this one how happy shoud I be"
Beauty thou sun shine of the passing hour
At once so lovley & so frail a flower
Gilt toy of life — with which all plays his part 275
Thou universal empress of the heart
Who woud not wish for hearts ease in thy room
One less delightfull or of longer bloom
Coud love while doating on thy looks so fair
But turn to days when time shall meddle there 280
& but reflect of its illfated spell
Pleasd to undo what nature did so well
To chill that cheek & all its sweets deform
Which youth had flushd so lucious & so warm
To dim those eyes & all their darts destroy 285
That brightning glows with misterys of joy
& damp those smiles that breath of silent bliss
To miss whose tasting seems a heaven to miss
Coud love but waken from its golden dreams
& see this shade which there a substance seems 290
Sure he woud think those heart aches & those sighs
Too dear a purchase for so false a prize
But love wears looks of heaven while it smiles
& Jockeys heart like others it beguiles
Was warmd too much at beautys blushing sun 295
To cool in reason when it once was won
Janes memory now claimd Jockeys every thought
Days came & went but little joy they brought

While abscence hopes & intermingling fears
Made hours to linger with the length of years 300
In vain the summer time his toil beguiles
With all her wild wood harmony & smiles
All disregarded Jockey passd em bye
& nothing claimd the notice of his eye
For Jockeys taste was not the vulgar hinds 305
He lookd oer nature with enlightend minds
& joyd like them ere love destroyd his rest
To be the wild woods solitary guest
To watch the brook boil oer its simmering tide
& crop the wild flower blooming by its side 310
To list the moaning of the winds & see
The grass in billows shadowing oer the lea
But love came on him with its burning bloom
& oer passt pleasures cast a sullen gloom
As silver moon beams in effulgence shed 315
Deepen nights darkness were they cannot spread
So joys behind him darkend seem & sour
Lost in the sweetness of a brighter flower
In vain did mirth excite him to forget
In vain at dances on the green he met 320
Were lovley faces might be seen again
Which but revivd the image of his Jane
Tho girls was there as fair & sweet to see
Were Jenny was not pleasure coud not be
Save the thrilld pleasures that to hope woud cling 325
For pains have pleasures when from love they spring
& had blind love been blest with eyes to see
What many pains might then as strangers be
What many souls that nature made to bind
Without a sigh or heart ache might be joind 330
How short with Jockey cares were doomd to dwell
Had he but known that Jinney lovd as well
Ah short had been his cares had he but known
Her heart dwelt there a neighbour with his own
For ever since the day he passd her door 335
She deemd it earnest what she guessd before

& expectations every now & then
Woud warm in hopes to see him once agen
Shed often provd a strangers forward gaze
& met with men impertinent to praise 340
But Jockeys manners thoughts coud ill reveal
& still warmd notions which she lovd to feel
To see her once then ramble to her home
Sure somthing urgd him & enticd to come
While with uneasy doubts her fears was free 345
To hint such notions might mistaken be
Which often urgd a mellancholy sigh
To check her blushing hopes when raisd too high
Jane in these reveries pursud her way
With lonley silence many a market day 350
Nor ever coud the loneley lovley spot
Were Jockey stood be wanderd bye forgot
As of[t] as thro the gate she went or came
A sigh & look woud busy memory claim
& passing bye hopes oft her bosom burnd 355
That she might meet him as she home returnd
But hopes decievd her still & many a day
With lonley thoughts she went her lonley way
For neer seemd spot so loan shed seen as yet
As that were abscent Jockey first was met 360
& neer shone suns so sadly to her eye
As shone that morning when he passd her bye
& even home had now no bliss to spare
Love claimd her heart & care pursued her there
Beneath the eldern she was heard no more 365
Toil making light with singing as before
In melancholly speed days went & came
Her hopes was doubtful & her peace the same
The laughing pleasures that was such before
Was now in mourning & coud please no more 370
The song of birds that usd to urge her own
Reminded now what changes she had known
The blooming flowers that usd to please her eye
Now livd as proofs of pleasures that were bye

Toil turnd a burthen — shoyness ill consceald 375
The painfull feelings that such ways reveald
Now night & morn in silence she was seen
With folded arms to soodle down the green
No flower enticd her as she sought the cow
& woodbines wreathd neglected round the bough 380
While round her path the lambs woud often stand
Bleating complaints of her neglecting hand
But fancyd joys that to the future cling
Gleamd oft like sunshine thro the clouds in spring
& hopes were budding with a future day 385
That now & then half drove despair away
Some weeks to come a village feast woud be
When Jinney hopd the strangers face to see
Twas from her cottage scarcley half a mile
& might fullwell such artless thought beguile 390
Sure if hed notions as she hopd he might
Hed neer miss coming to the dance at night
& if he lovd her as she hopd he did
Such chance to meet from him woud not be hid
So Jinney judgd & to her hearts delight 395
Found all her wishes when it came was right
Nor fruitless was her prayers for on that day
Suns shone as wishd & rain kept far away
Paths were as clean as wishes coud desire
Nor wet nor dew to sully her attire 400
Her sundays best that eve she hastend on
With warmest hopes to win & to be won
A gay straw hat with ribbons on the peak
Of roseys hue like that upon her cheek
Oer her white bosom loves delicious bed 405
A silken hankerchief was loosly spread
That hid its swelling sweets in carless ways
& still left room for armorous eyes to gaze
A fine new gown round boddice lightly bracd
Flowd to the wind & claspd her slender waist 410
While dust to shun she held it to her side
Disclosing beautys which she seemd to hide

A slender ancle clad in stocking white
Which swelld in sweet propo[r]tions out of sight
& jet black was her shoe & polishd high 415
Tyd wi black ribbon in a gracful tye
Thus in her best on tiptoe to be seen
With bosom warmd its hopes & doubts between
She left her cot half weand from lingering care
To seek the dance in hopes to meet him there 420
& sure enough as wishd 'spectations came
For Jockeys hopes that evening were the same
& at an earlier hour from toil releasd
He drest him smart & hastnd to the feast
Anxious & hopfull as he pac'd the street 425
Neath every hat the lovly face to meet
& to the dance with hopes unprovd as yet
He went & lookd & there the face was met
Tween hopes & fears his courage flutterd chill
Then warmd agen but doubted strongly still 430
But looks he venturd & woud looks repeat
& venturd near Jane blushd but kept her seat
Emboldnd thus love from its silence broke
Seizing her hand that trembld while he spoke
He hopd to be his partner shed consent 435
Nor deem him rude when rudness was not meant
"Yes" beat her bosom mid its throbs & sighs
Fond to reveal but modest to disguise
Her eyes met his a smile half blushd to view
& glowd more tenderer as he urgd anew 440
His suit he movd with fonder freedom still
& Jenny rose as if against her will
Half shrinking from herself with fears & bliss
Neer urgd till now & now as urgd amiss
& tho her coyness downward turnd the while 445
From Jockeys view she coud not hide the smile
Which gave consent & plainly told the rest
That hopes half speeded & woud soon be blest
For he as yet had venturd not to move
His suit so far to tell her it was love 450

But speaking eyes have language in their way
Whose looks oft seem to chide the tongues delay
& Jinney often neath her bonnets brim
When others lookd not turnd to gaze on him
& oh so sweet so languishing the while 455
Tween blushing coyness & a dimpling smile
They plainly askd him ere they turnd aside
To kiss those lips that reddnd to be tryd
& press that bosom hand had never prest
& wisper love & put all doubts to rest 460
But Jockey perseverd with modesty
Nor urgd too forward fear of being too free
He led her down the dance with hopes beguild
& often nipt her hand & often smild
Till evenings end proclaimed night too nigh 465
That left its admonitions with a sigh
On more then Jenney when with many a maid
The dance must stop & parents be obey'd
She sought her shawl which caution loosley threw
Around her neck to guard against the dew 470
& left the dance & for her home sojournd
But turnd a look on Jockey as she turnd
Who sued to walk as guardian by her side
Nor seemd she to consent nor yet denyd
Still Jockey urgd successes to pursue 475
Took her white arm & brushd the nightly dew
Offering assistance oer each stile & brook
& felt the joy to see it kindly took
Adventuring often on their lonly way
By closer hints his meaning to convey 480
Oft bringing memory round her mind to try
Of that first morning when she past him bye
To prove if he had aught of fondness won
& livd with her as she with him had done
While Jennys meek & modest sighs conseald 485
Her warm consent to fondness thus reveald
& pity tis that hours that bring us joy
Shoud lend that wings which follows to destroy

Time seems with grief to loiter & delay
But flyes from hearts that wishes him to stay 490
Soon came their journeys end how much too soon
Tho quite contrary gleamd the mounting moon
That seemd that night to gallop on his way
& hinted now theyd made too much delay
Abruptly on their sight the cottage rose 495
& loves tales stopt when warmest to disclose
For raptures now did all his fears efface
& love was shown in many a warm embrace
But hours of meeting sweet as they begin
Have parting ones that claim too near a kin 500
Glimmering thro Jinneys window light did burn
That showd her parents waited her return
Fled was those modest hours she usd to keep
& night was slumbering in its soundest sleep
So they must part — still Jockey lingerd nigh 505
& sigh'd complaints which Jenney coud but sigh
Whatever wishes in her breast might burn
Jane must retire & Jockey must return
She dare not risk the hazard or the blame
To take a stranger to a chiding dame 510
So part they must — but Jockey sued agen
For one more kiss one minute more & then
Prest her soft hand & much against his will
Sighd "Jane farewell" — & held her prisoner still
Till thoughts of friends wakd innoscent alarms 515
& forcd young Jinney from her lovers arms
"Then as we must — farewell" exclaimd the swain
"Till sundays leisure & Im here again"
She sighd consent — he viewd his lonly ways
Then turnd agen as wishing new delays 520
But Jinney timid with the depth of night
Opend the door & vanishd from his sight
Where the old folks her glad approach did wait
& urgd their questions of her being so late
But kept it secret what they guessd the while 525
& heard excuses tween a frown & smile

They knew their daughters manners up to this
Nor yet had doubted of her doing amiss
Her father hinted his advice in time
Tho well he knew hed done the little crime 530
& while he guessd the late hour savourd love
He check'd the dame nor venturd to reprove
So all was right—Jane dreemd about the swain
& counted hours when they shoud meet again
& surley nights did never seem so slow 535
To bring the sun & bid the sun to go
Then those that passd between with lagging feet
That eves first meeting & the next to meet
At length it came & Jane oft turnd her eye
Upon the window watching passers bye 540
Whose blushing hopes was startld into joys
At every footstep or approaching noise
When ere the gate clapt creaking on the moor
She left her book & venturd to the door
For Jane had long been taught her god to fear 545
& tho there was no place of worship near
She knew what duty on that day requird
& always took her bible as desird
Still Jinneys bible had not power to chide
Loves tempting charm with innoscence its guide 550
Oft did she think of more then what she read
& towards the window often turnd her head
Nor did she long those cheating hopes pursue
Ere Jockeys presence provd his promise true
In thoughtfull mood she markd him on the moor 555
Taking the path that winded to the door
Were soon a fearfull rap warnd Jane to move
Her best excuse & intercede for love
Let this suffice she told the simple tale
& told it true as better to prevail 560
They cooly heard it but denyd him not
So he half doubtfull enterd in the cott
Were Jenny smiling as she set the chair
Provd he by one was doubly welcome there

& soon his modest unasuming ways 565
Urgd the old folks' opinion in his praise
With each new visit grew increasd esteem
Proving sincere what first might doubtfull seem
& oft he came & many a sabbath day
They toyd with bliss & lovd its hours away 570
Oft seeking pleasure that retirement yields
In peacful rambles round the silent fields
Unseen while wandering in each lonley dell
Unheard while talking what they lovd to tell
Sitting to rest on sunny bauk or stile 575
& kindred feelings as they sat the while
Explaining there — how abscence gave them pain
& joys encreasd when thus they met again
& oft while wandering thus in summers hours
Hed match her beauty with surrounding flowers 580
Comparing some to blushes on her cheek
Some to her lips when tingd with ruddier streak
& those more sweet & whiter then the rest
That to her breath & this her swelling breast
& then half shrinking from his ardent gaze 585
Hed snatch a kiss as purchase for his praise
Thus hours were spent & time as passing bye
Kept knitting love with closer tenderer tye
No change creating as is oft the case
Kindling fresh fondness for a stranger face 590
With Jockeys feelings change woud ill agree
Tho he saw faces that was sweet to see
Yet warmest fancy always rose at will
& picturd abscent Jinny fairer still
By frequent visits love at length was led 595
To bring up questions when they might be wed
Their friends consent was all that left delay
They askd & had it & they fixd the day
The friends of Jane had learnd her how to live
& Jockeys friends had little else to give 600
For tho to desent living they attaind
Riches by them was neither prizd nor gaind

Land they possest but niggard was the soil
& just returned a recompence for toil
Virtue & industry their choice requir'd 605
Them Jane possest & they was all desir'd
So all was fixt & soon the morning came
When Jane shoud be a bride & change her name
& Jockeys heart that morn with bliss was warm
But Jenney trembld as she took his arm 610
Tho gay companions cheer'd her journying on
& soon the church proclaimd their journey done
Where Jenny enterd chiding what she felt
& meekly down before the vicar knelt
Who tyd that nott & not without its sigh 615
Which all save death is puzzld to untye
With Jockey still all cares was set aside
He lookd with raptures on his lovley bride
Whose fondness coud not overcome her fears
She smild returning but she smild in tears 620
& when her husband urgd the reason why
She coud not tell — unless it was for joy
First love how sweet ah woud it longer last
Tho time remembers it when felt & past
Tis but a shadow of a substance gone 625
A setting sunbeam to a rising one
Hope feeds on joys imagination gives
Which in this world as pictures only lives
Attempt it, oft half care half joy we find
Posses it quite cares often left behind 630
Love like the Sensitive oft proves as such
Fair to the eye & withering at the touch
Revealing cares that marriage vows await
Which brings repentence that is brought too late
But Jane & Jockey little had to do 635
With such as yet while honey moons was new
Bright in their infancy of rapturd gleams
No cares were yet to cloud such lovley dreams
First love is theirs — what else may interpose
Here they are blest & here the tale shall close 640

Going to the Fair

Gay rose the morn fulfilling many a prayer
Of anxious maids — the day was Topal Fair
The month was may the meadows they were green
& full of flowers tho paths were far from clean
Moistened by showers that frequent tho not long 5
Fell & were done ere linnets could their song
That now by crowds in every thicket sung
& from the mill dam up the Heron sprung
In every field larks twittered oer the grain
As happy twas the fair so thought the swain 10
Who hastened oer his labour to get free
By times the pleasures of the fair to see
The very air breathed joy & all the May
To such appeared in joyouance with the day
As if the fair had put their pleasures on 15
Thus merry minds shape raptures from their own
In ivy bowers wood piegons sat to coo
& smooth voiced cuckoos muttered as they flew
Free smiled the daisey from dull nights embrace
Flushed with his dewy kisses on its face 20
The sun was peeping oer the spreading rows
Of dark green elms alive with busy crows
& round the Lodge that darkened neath their shade
Loud was the strife that pigs & poultry made
A farm house now tho once a moated hall 25
As loud too farmer Thriftys morning call
"Come up boys up" re-echoed thro the Lodge
Where last to bed & first to rise was Hodge
Who heard the unwelcome shout mid yawns & sighs
& spent some minutes to unclose his eyes 30
Yet up he must to fetch his horses now
They needed corn & waiting lay the plough
& mornings toil must needs be finished soon
As all had leave to join the fair at noon
So up Hodge got & soodled down the lane 35
Hirpling like one whose joints was stiff with pain

Tho urged by many a call till out of sight
To mend his pace & not be out till night
& Simon foremost of the servant clan
Who next the master ruled as master man 40
Was more than anxious to perform his part
Who stript already stopt his song to start
As love & hope with mingling fear & glee
Burnt every thought with madness to be free
Mary a maid whose fame was in her face 45
Who lived his partner in his last years place
& now tho distant from him many a mile
Her former fondness cheered his present toil
For she had vowed last martinmass when they
For their new places parted wide away 50
That come what would — on the returning Fair
She'd come to see her friends & meet him there
So Simons hopes who painted her as come
Burnt till they grew all rebels to their home
Forcing his heart on fancys wings to wend 55
In thought already at its journeys end
His mind all night on thoughts with dull delay
Its parting waited wide awake for day
& now the day had come he waited on
To end his mornings labour & begone 60
While mingling hopes unsatisfied desires
With their warm gushes & blood boiling fires
Scarce gave him time — so anxious to pursue
Even to think of what he had to do
By kindness he had bought in seasons past 65
The love of Mary which he hoped would last
Who young & blushing was & sweet to see
Yet not like gaudy roses on the tree
For beauty blazed not in her face yet there
A twilight splendour owned her more then fair 70
Illumned by many a mellancholly smile
That taste while gazing might believe the while
The pastoral muse did in her beauty shine
Such as might warm far better songs than mine

The voice of woods & streams was in her looks 75
& wise she seemed tho ignorant of books
Her hair was swarthy brown & soft of hue
As the sweet gloom that falls with evens dew
That on her fine white forhead did divide
In the triumphant negligence of pride 80
Her eyes were dark but they wore lights to shine
That love adores & poets call divine
& her cheeks summer blooms wore hues the while
Of loves soft innoscence without its guile
& on the pouting of her amorous lip 85
Where love delicious nectar longed to sip
Beauty sat throned in that bewitching spell
That love adores & language cannot tell
Where charms triumphant made each gazer pay
Heart aches for looking ere he turned away 90
& so did Simons but the smiles that cured
Paid more then double for the pain endured
For in loves views to win her kind regard
He milked — & every sunday swept the yard
That she might on her errands safely go 95
Nor soil the gloss jet of her sunday shoe
& from the stack a faggot every night
He threw his Marys morning fire to light
Nay did all toils her sundays had to do
When she had on a garment that was new 100
& feared with thorns to tear or dirt to soil
While love was all the payment for his toil
By all these deeds he strove his love to show
Nor was she backward what they meant to know
& tho she shrieked to shun a stolen kiss 105
A chance to meet his smile shed never miss
& oft for syllabubs for cream she crept
When mistress gossiped & the master slept
& slove the cellar key from off the nail
Above her masters chair to steal him ale 110
While in those favoured hours most like to speed
Simon had sued & Mary had agreed

Live where they might or fair or foul the weather
Theyd meet this morning at the fair together
Altho six lingering months since then had now 115
Spread in between warm love to cool that vow
Altho six lingering miles with dreary view
Stretched loves frail chain — still he believed her true
At length came Hodge with trouble in his speed
For when with quicker pace he did proceed 120
Bad news was sure the herald of his tale
To say a portion of his job did fail
& now he stopt his song ere nigh to bawl
Of gaps new broke & horses vanished all
For he seemed joyed to find them all astray 125
Wishing no doubt theyd neer be found that day
A truce from plough to rest each weary limb
Was more then fairs or holidays to him
Simon in silence like a statue stood
Dire dissapointment curdled up his blood 130
His hopes & holiday all seemed as done
While farmer thrifty bade them search till noon
Sending out heralds famed for swifter speed
Than Hodge grown needless in the time of need
When soon the horses all were found but one 135
& Dobbin oftenest to transgress was gone
Dobbin a horse well known for miles around
In every village & in every pound
Altho so tame at toil that boys might guide
& childern walk uninjured by his side 140
When loose from geers he roved as freedoms mate
Hed find all gaps & open every gate
& if aught sweet beyond his pasture grew
No fence so thick but he would blunder thro'
His youth from gipseys did these tricks recieve 145
With them he toiled & worked his wits to live
Bare roads he traced all day with nought to bite
Then stole with them to stacks to feed at night
Tho now a better life was Dobbins lot
Well fed & fat youths tricks he neer forgot 150

Still gaps were broke & dobbin bore the blame
Still stacks were pulled & Dobbin felt no shame
If fifty partners in his pasture lay
Dobbin was safe to lead them all astray
& yet a better horse all did alow 155
Was never yoked to waggon or to plough
Old farmer thrifty now with vengance ripe
Cursed & laid down half smoaked his morning pipe
Vowing old Dobbins tricks would loose his crop
Of corn if thus whole days they forced to stop 160
The harrow — & then threw his hands behind him
"If hes above ground curse him we will find him"
& Simon as the safest to succeed
Was posted off & tho to urge his speed
A flaggon of the best ere he did start 165
Was drawn that burnt like brandy round his heart
But nothing cheered it for his hopes was crost
& chance of meeting Mary seemed as lost
Yet he brushed onward on his doubtful rout
With best leg foremost to find Dobbin out 170
Muttering his threats in angers blustering tones
How he would thrash the wanderers lazy bones
Whittling a monstrous cudgel while he spoke
Proving therebye he did not mean to joke
Alas for Dobbin sore will be his back 175
If Simon finds him & he marks his track
For faithless dews his blundering steps betrayed
Oer close & field in crooked marks displayed
But the kind sun that smiles on all below
Was Dobbins friend tho Simon was his foe 180
Drying the tell tale dew from off the grass
Leaving the ploughman to proceed by guess
Who asked of almost every one he met
Searched in each pound & neer the wiser yet
Measuring his shadow every now & then 185
To guess the hour then hurried on agen
While Marys smiles & promise & the fair
Rose oer all hopes & drove them to despair

Search where he might enquire of whom he would
Dobbin was missing as if lost for good 190
For he was reckoned cunning & at least
Had more of reason then a common beast
Seeking such secret spots from summer skys
As if he hid from toil as well as flies
This Simon knew & searched in every spot 195
Where he might hide but yet had hidden not
So on he searched & cursed & searched again
Muttering the while his threatning oaths in vain
Laying to Dobbins tramp in reckless strife
The loss of love & happiness for life 200
While short his shadow grew & shifted on
Untill it tokened half the day was gone
& what was worse the hour when at the gate
Mary for Simons coming was to wait
When he had told her last & vowed as how 205
That spot should sink ere he would break his vow
That vow was broke — at least the time expired
When Mary was to wait as love desired
& wait she did for half the morning there
Where two paths met the high road to the fair 210
She left her fathers cot before the time
To make her lover wait appeared a crime
"Decietful man" doubt burnt hopes taper dim
She sighed & muttered "I may wait for him"
"Here I may stand in doubt the morning long 215
"Altho he knows he never thinks it wrong
"Last night I came six weary miles in vain
"Cheered with the thoughts of seeing him again
"My mothers love could ill my absence spare
"But without Simon I was restless there" 220
So sighed the maid as oer the stile she bent
& sighed & onward to the fair she went
While every noise that floated in the wind
Would make her pause & turn a look behind
For Simons haloo she would list & look 225
Loitering & musing to be overtook

Altho still cheated — down each narrow lane
At every turn she'd stop & wait again
Till tired with hopes excuses for delay
The rose bud in her bosom dyed away 230
Which there was placed new graces to reveal
Or more for Simons tempted hands to steal
But Simon came not & the withered rose
Was the first omen sorrows to disclose
Stung with the void of abscence to the fair 235
Hopes curdled all to malice — & when there
To loose her thoughts she struggled to be gay
Passing in freakish whims the merry day
Mocking gay feelings that had small akin
To the perplexitys that lurked within 240
Changing her nature & in freedoms ways
Smiled as if courting amorous eyes to gaze
Taking with willing hand in merry cue
The glass to kiss from every youth she knew
Each proffered fairing too was freely taen 245
She cracked the nutts & threw the shells again
Resolved to change her old love for a new
& leave off Simon deemed no longer true
Yet half unconscious of the looks she raised
She blushed & seemed to wonder why they praised 250
While Footman Tim in his gilt gaudy suit
Tapping with pride his cane upon his boot
Grown bold with ale nipt up in smirking glee
& rudely made her welcome to his knee
Soon from his silken purse his cash was flung 255
& crown by crown upon the table rung
For every groat & een a penny paid
This purse & all this silver was displayed
The while he sat he'd chink his cash about
To let folks know his pockets wa'n't without 260
Tween thumb & finger oft he swung his cane
In haughty grace then sipt his glass again
Still leaving dregs at bottom to throw down
To show how fashion acted from a clown

& more in Marys presence to display 265
A careless waste as heeding not the pay
Full oft unbidden out his watch was taen
To show the hour but more to show the chain
& off his gloves were pulled his nails to bite
With vain excuse to show his hands were white 270
While open flew his waist coat at the chin
Crimpt frills displaying & a golden pin
To raise his consequence in vulgar eyes
& win the girls to think a blank a prize
Mary seemed hurt yet suffered to be held 275
Bearing the seat with patience while compelled
& Simon now with weary feet & mind
Pursuing Dobbin whom he could not find
Gave up the hunt his master heard the tale
& swore yet paid him with a horn of ale 280
Saying as morn was bye he well could spare
Them all — so all made ready for the fair
His Ash plant Simon in his hand had got
Yet paused in doubt half willing & half not
Beside the door with kerchief smoothening down 285
The ruffled nap upon his beavers crown
Then starting off then still foreboding doubt
Dark fears strong impulse made him pause about
Sweet was the day & sunny gleamed the weather
While sheep loud bleating called their lambs together 290
"Craik" went the Land rail in the wind waved grain
Whom idle schoolboys hearing chased in vain
In Simons mind the noise bespoke his fate
He thought it muttered he was all too "late"
"Chewsit" the Pewit screamed in swopping wews 295
"Chuse it" said Simon I know whom to chuse
Thus neer a bird could sing but Simons cares
Shaped it to somthing of his own affairs
& while he whiped the moisture from his brow
Fear chilled his spirit with his broken vow 300
& soon must love like lifes deciet decide
How nearly joys & sorrows are allied

The day was swiftly wasting with the wear
& some few girls were coming from the fair
Who left gay mirth & all his noisey crew 305
Not without sighs their evening jobs to do
& he when met got many a laughing look
Full loud their fears were urged to cross the brook
Knocking their pattens when no dirt was near
& finding danger where no danger were 310
Signals to urge the aid of Simons hand
But such he could or would not understand
He hurried by them all & would not stay
To ask a question or salute the day
Tho screams & shouts alternate rung behind 315
Raising their wanton ecchoes on the wind
He never once turned oer his arm to see
If they got oer or in the brook not he
His thoughts already at their journeys end
Left him no time on trifles to attend 320
With patten rings the path was thickly cut
Where fancy painted Marys nimble foot
In many a printing mark as on before
Which burnt his thoughts & hastened him the more
At length the noisey fair assailed his ear 325
Great grew his hope but greater grew his fear
& as he crushed among the crowds when there
His eyes dare scarcely wander oer the fair
Lest he — for fear was busy to alarm
Should see his Mary on anothers arm 330
& as his spirits worn in feeble guise
Needed the boldness barley stout supplies
He sought the ale house where by fear repelled
He scarce dare credit what his eyes beheld
When in a corner full of out ward glee 335
He saw his Mary on anothers knee
He turned away nor would his looks repeat
She turned as white as death but kept her seat
For well she thought his carelessness foretold
He for a new love had forsook the old 340

While he with far more cause for dark distrust
Thought all was over & his actions just
& tho he could not stifle without pain
His love he thought it useless to explain
So sat in silence as if none the while 345
Was worth the notice of a word or smile
Yet as poor captives oft in hopeless plight
Look thro their bars on liberty & light
So did his eyes beneath his beavers brim
Steal looks on Mary half unknown to him 350
While lifting up when not athirst the quart
To drown the sigh fast swelling from his heart
& Mary smiling struggled to be gay
Tho dissapointment turned her cheek to clay
& eat like cankers every rose away 355
The deepest sorrow hath no tongue but steals
Signs from the heart betraying what it feels
Sighs come at deeper eloquence than speech
& tears touch chords that language cannot reach
—While footman Tim was busy with his tale 360
& toasting Mary oer each draught of ale
Simon as able to behold no more
Emptied his quart & hurried to the door
To seek amusement in the noise & rout
Within the fair & keep old memorys out 365
But all were blanks & every wish was vain
& search for peace still added more to pain
The showmans shouts which wonder yearly brings
The huge hung pictures of outlandish things
Where grinning tigers wavered in the wind 370
Raising more wonders than they hid behind
The merry fool that would his speeches make
Till at the sport old womens sides would ache
These without pleasure now he sauntered bye
& only turned a careless ear or eye 375
& weary with the frolic & the fun
He sauntered homeward ere the fair was done
While as in melancholly mood he went

In mutterings loud he gave his sorrows vent
"Is it for this" he said & turned behind 380
As if mistrustful of the listening wind
"Is it for this I watched till church was oer
Her hens & scoldings from the parson bore
Hunting the eggs all churchtime thro the day
That none should scold her cause they laid away 385
Is it for this my credit all at stake
& even life I ventured for her sake
When in the orchard while she milked her cows
I stole & clambered to the topmost boughs
To reach the reddest apple plumb or pear 390
For no more payment than a smile could spare
Smiles feed young love to madness & beguiles
So Ive rued sorely since I lived on smiles
In this same close which brings up happier hours
On sundays when we brushed these self same flowers 395
When glossy slippers did her feet bedeck
I took my kerchief even from my neck
To whipe off lingering drops of by gone showers
Or maybe tears from crushed & broken flowers
& dust that would their glossy hues oer cast 400
Powdered from king cups shaken as we past
But whats the use to bring up things gone bye
My best I did & the worst served am I"
Here Simon stopt for loud upon his ear
Stole merry voices fast approaching near 405
From many laughing home returning groups
Not sad like Simon under broken hopes
But wild with joy glad frolicked many a lass
On ploughmans arms light skipping thro the grass
Old men & women too with ale inspired 410
Felt young again & laughed till they were tired
While childern stooped & shouted by their sides
To see their shadows take such antique strides
As mocking the old dames who danced & sung
With aprons spread as nimble as the young 415
Simon right anxious for the nights disguise

Hurried along to hide from meddling eyes
While low the sun in evenings mellow light
Behind the meadow bridges sunk from sight
Yet as if loath to leave the merry crew 420
Peeped thro the arches in a last adieu
Simon tho filled with thoughts reflecting pain
Could not but turn to see it peep again
Remembering at the sight in happier days
How Mary stood that self same thing to praise 425
What sorrowful delights such dreams bequeath
What golden feelings clad in memorys wreath
Past reccolections in our bosoms move
That once were hopes attendants upon love
& Simon een in sorrow felt a joy 430
From memorys past that nothing could destroy
But such are reveries that will not last
They come like thoughts & ere we muse are past
Hopes change like summer clouds from shape to shape
Setting the restless fancies all agape 435
& painting joys as beautiful & fair
Till all disolves into the common air
So Simon proved it as he onward sped
Who soon as home went supperless to bed
& tho at toil next day he bawled & sung 440
Twas but to smother how his heart was wrung
His mind still laboured over past affairs
& strove in vain to get the start of cares
While hope proposed a medicine for pain
Making it up to see her once again 445
Resolving if next sunday should be fine
To look oer all & ere he would resign
Loves all hed go & clear himself from wrong
& tell what kept him from the fair so long
For he believed & did his follys scoff 450
That Mary fancied he had left her off
& at the fair in hurt loves jealous whim
To be revenged took up with Footman Tim
Thus Simon thought & often stopt his song

To curse lost Dobbin that had caused the wrong 455
Soon Sunday came & to make worse the matter
Rain drops from off the eves did quickly patter
He heard it while abed for sorrow aches
Around the heart & haunts it while it wakes
Sad sad he listened to the pattering sound 460
While every plash left hope a deeper wound
Ere the gray cock nights watch man did supprise
Nights startled sleep & bid the sun to rise
& up he got & with an anxious eye
From out the window looked upon the sky 465
That darkly glowered as if it meant to last
Raining away so thickly & so fast
That every drop made bubbles as they fell
In the mossed duck pond & uncovered well
While brimming ruts did headlong journeys go 470
As if like springs they ever meant to flow
Vain hope what is it as its sun declines
A balm on which the sick heart feeds & pines
& many a heart from whence its rapture came
Is nothing now but memory & a name 475
Victims of love that cheated them too long
Sunk to the burthen of a mournful song
But Simon tho perplext felt not that smart
So deep that endeth in a broken heart
Of ruder mould was he & ruder form 480
That like the oak grows stubborn in a storm
Not like the weaker sort that bend & sigh
& at a frown cling to despair & die
The rain it ceased at noon the sky looked thro
The breaking clouds in many a patch of blue 485
As breaks the thick ice in a sudden thaw
Showing the bottom of the brook below
When Simon instantly from off the nail
His bran new beaver reached & without fail
Brushed oer the plashy fields & dripping stiles 490
Careless of shortening day & lengthening miles
For Marys smiles would be to him as light

& make een sunshine of the darkest night
& so they ought for ere he reached the place
The sun sunk low & bade good night apace 495
& while the spire peeped oer the woodland bough
He stopt to whipe the moisture from his brow
Asking a shepherd where the farm might be
About the town where Mary lived — & he
Scarce raised him on his elbow from his lare 500
& holding out his sheep hook halooed "there"
When on his greedy ear her well known voice
Ecchoed amain & made his heart rejoice
As in a milking nook she called her cows
When on he sped & hid among the boughs 505
Of black thorn growing in disorder near
The sad revealings of her mind to hear
For grief in solitude will tell tho vain
Its sorrows to itself to ease the pain
That stifling silence round the heart inurned 510
Simon thus much by self experience learned
So down he dropt amid the thickets shade
To list unseen the unsuspecting maid
Staining his garments with the bruising grass
For he thought little of his sunday dress 515
Nor was his expectation long decieved
Her sighs soon told him how her heart was grieved
& while the brook in mingling mutterings ran
She milked & thus her sad complaint began
"Fye Simon fye to seem to love so true 520
"Your heedless follys know not what they do
"My hearts nigh broken with his broken vow
"I feel so sad I scarce can milk my cow
"Yet none will free me from my sunday toil
"So I must milk & sunday gowns must spoil 525
"& spoil they may — I feel in loves despair
"Few are the number I shall live to wear
"Simons unkindness made all pleasures vain
"& left me wounds that cannot heal again
"Ungrateful man to do as he hath done 530

"To take my pails that I the dirt might shun
"& lay fresh stones when eer the brook was high
"That I might cross in safety & be dry
"Then all at once to fling me from his mind
"Nor een on memory turn a look behind 535
"Around me as he did like Ivy cling
"& then to spurn me like a poison thing
"Dear what a terror of suspence Im in
"My heart een heaves my bosom to my chin
"& swelled with troubles that I could not see 540
"Unpins my kerchief as it would be free
"But sad to think of that can never be
"I felt no joy in fussy Footman Tim
"Twas down right malice made me notice him
"& vain I tryed to yield & he to win 545
"For love & malice claim but small akin
"False Simon first my foolish heart beguiled
"& to none else will it be reconsiled
"Would I could pluck his memory from my mind
"Just as a dew drop trembles from the wind 550
"O dear I cannot for my heart must own
"The pain it feeleth to be left alone
"To weep unseen & all unheard to sigh
"Left all to silent loneliness am I
"Save that the Robin every time I come 555
"Peepeth & makes me welcome to his home
"Leaving in neighbouring bush its mossy nest
"To visit & invite me for its guest
"Perk nimble thing were I but half as free
"& half as happy I might sing with thee 560
"Thy love proves true but mine was false & bad
"& that which makes thee happy makes me sad
"—Well foolish griefs are follys many say
"& longs the night that never looks for day
"Well if the roads are bad & love unkind 565
"Ive got my pattens still so never mind
"Thank heaven Im neither blind or lame to need
"A arm to lean on or a guide to lead

"Yet will my heart be sad" so said her sighs
As she turned up her apron to her eyes 570
 Simon heard all & from his hiding place
Rushed out & caught her in his hearts embrace
Cheered was his soul forgetting former toil
Glad as the hope that meets a lovers smile
Warmth did away the bashfulness of love 575
Leaving no pause to fear she might reprove
Alarm in her denials put to strife
& waked past pleasures into sudden life
Lost in his arms loves reverie beguiles
& kisses dry her sorrows into smiles 580
Till burning joy that speech to each denied
Did into reasons cooler light subside
Then Simon up & told her all & how
Misfortunes fell & made him break his vow
& laid it all to Dobbin who at large 585
Unfound remained as heedless of the charge
He told what kept him from the fair so long
She heard with joy yet grieved she judged so wrong
& from that night both pledged eternal love
Leaving the rest to him who rules above 590
& Simon when they parted in delight
Could not help singing tho twas sunday night
& sung so loud too on his homeward way
That birds awoke & thought it must be day
& day it was before he reached the farm 595
Where gaping wonder with enquirey warm
On tiptoe stood to question his delay
Where he had been & why he chose to stay
But silence whom no bribe can force to speak
Kept close her lips & left them still to seek 600
Time went on smooth & gaily with him now
& glad as larks that sung him to his plough
He toiled & sung & labour seemed as nought
While Marys smiles had share of every thought
Save now & then as oer his memory crost 605
The thought of Dobbin whom all reckoned lost

& many a week went bye & grew age
To two whole months of mystery & then
With ribs nigh bare & shoulders gauled & sore
One morn they found him at the stable door 610
Waiting as not forgot the accustomed corn
Which he was wont to share of every morn
Hodge spied him first & with a joyous shout
Cried "heres old dobbin" — when from breakfast out
Came all & joy in every face did burn 615
Pleased as are mothers when their sons return
One clapped his sides one did his memory bless
While Dobbins looks bespoke his hearts distress
Low hung his lip nor in his former way
Did he give signs of frolic or of play 620
Yet when his name was called with freshened will
He prickt his ears as if he knew it still
The Farmer cursed the thieves he hoped to track
& clapped old Dobbin as right welcome back
& gave him extra corn & extra rest 625
Till he grew fat & frolic as the best
When he his former fame revived again
For breaking gaps & getting in the grain
& oft in after years with memorys mirth
Simon raised laughter round his cottage hearth 630
With tales of Dobbins strange eventful life
When happy Mary had become his wife
Who often laughed while in his elbow chair
He told the cause that kept him from the fair
& all the pains then felt now banished hence 635
Since Marys love had made them reccompence
Nay kisses now he claimed back debts to pay
& thus the winters evening wore away
Blessed each with each like birds in summer weather
Light was the chain that joined their hearts together 640

Valentine Eve

Young girls grow eager as the day retires
& smile & whisper round their cottage fires
Listning for noises in the dusky street
For tinkling latches & for passing feet
The prophecys of coming joys to hark 5
Of wandering lovers stealing thro' the dark
Dropping their valentines at beautys door
With hearts & darts & love knots littered oer
"Aye" said a gossip by a neighbours hearth
While the young girls popt up in tittering mirth 10
To hear the door creek with heart jumping signs
& footsteps hastening bye & valentines
Drop rustling on the floor — "aye aye" she said
(As they kept back & smiled oer what they read)
Your fine love letters might be worth your smiles 15
If 'stead of coming from some creeping giles
Rich lovers sent them as it once befell
To one young maiden I remember well
Tho Madam Meers now lives at oakley hall
With coach & four & footmen at her call 20
Her father was none else than farmer Ling
& she plain Kate before she wore a ring
Tho I began about the valentine
The starting subject Ill awhile resign
But hear with patience & yell quickly learn 25
For Ill haste on & take it up in turn
When the poor irish from their country rove
& like scotch cattle throng the road in droves
To seek the profits which the harvest brings
At that same season to old farmer Lings 30
A stranger came but not of foreign blood
He spoke plain english & his looks was good
& hired himself for toil the season thro
At any jobs the harvest had to do
& tho he seemed as merry as the clowns 35
He neer was noisey like such vulgar lowns

& when he heard them urge a vulgar joke
At passing maids he neither laughd nor spoke
But while he saw the blush their rudeness made
His manners seemed their freedom to upbraid 40
For hed turn round a moment from his toil
& say "good morning" & would kindly smile
Tho dressed like them in jacket russet brown
His ways betrayed him better than a clown
& many a guess from rumours whispers fell 45
& gossips daily had new tales to tell
Some said he once had been a wealthy man
& from a bankrupts painful ruin ran
Others with far worse causes marked his flight
& taxed him with a forgers name out right 50
& tho he heard such whispers passing bye
Hed laugh but never stop to question why
Nor seemed offended think whatere he would
But always seemed to be in merry mood
Bad as folks thought him I was well aware 55
That he by one at least was welcome there
Who always mid their noisey idle prate
Would silent stand & that was rosey Kate
She seemed bewitched with his good mannered ways
& never spoke about him but to praise 60
She was the youngest daughter fair & gay
As flowers that open in the dews of May
Loves heart neer trembled at a sweeter face
When health & beauty courted its embrace
Nor lived a merrier girl beneath the sun 65
For romp & play when labours work was done
Wild as a Doe that over leapt the park
She'd laugh & play oer evenings games till dark
All noise & stir like an ill sitting hen
But shoy & timid in the sight of men 70
Her friends neer dreamed of what all else might see
His ways was plain as the "cross row" to me
When ere he caught her in her dissabille
Washing or aught – she ran as lovers will

Up stairs as quickly as she could from sight 75
To seek her glass & put her garments right
Anxious to meet him in her best attire
As he the more might love her & admire
& once at eve as we the cows did wait
He leaned beside her on the stackyard gate 80
& smiled & whispered as she stooped adown
To pull some burdocks from her sweeping gown
"Mary theres one whose thoughts when your away
"Always cling with you full as close as they
"Who hopes yet fears his growing love to name 85
"Lest you should throw it from you just the same"
She coloured like the fire & turned aside
But I saw quickly what her heart would hide
& up & told her when she milked at night
That be the harvest stranger who he might 90
A winning tongue neaths toils disguise was hid
That knew more manners then our farmers did
She laughd & said "aye so you love him then
But as for her shed no regard for men"
Tho such denials kept the secret worse 95
I took no heed but sanctioned her discourse
& when she dressed to walk on harvest eves
Spending an hour to glean among the sheaves
Things were to others eyes full often seen
That she'd more errands than the one to glean 100
She always follow'd in the strangers toil
Who oft would stop to wet his hook & smile
& loose when none percieved from out his hand
Some wheat ears now & then upon the land
& oft when running from a sudden shower 105
Or leaving off to take their beavering hour
He always from the rest would linger last
To leave a smile & greet her as he past
All that had any sense to use their eyes
Might easy guess beneath the thin disguise 110
Like to the burr about the moon at night
It seems to covert but still leaves it light

& sure enough he was a handsome swain
One any maiden had been proud to gain
Een I have often envied Kittys place 115
& felt the heart ache at his smiling face
For when I passed him he would always smile
& often took my milk pail oer a stile
Jeering us both of sweethearts in our play
Tho nothing but in good behaviours way 120
He said to me — yet without shame I say't
I thought myself as fine a wench as Kate
Dark as the strangers mystery were his ways
He wandered round the field on sabbath days
& left to vulgar minds the noisey town 125
Nor made a partner of a fellow clown
Traceing the wood tracks over grown with moss
Or with heath rabbits winding thro the goss
& oft neath black thorn shadows by the brook
Was seen by shepherds musing oer a book 130
& in his button holes was always seen
Wild flowers — that in his rambles he would glean
Folks often marvelled at each seeming whim
What we thought weeds seemd best of flowers with him
The ragged robbin by the runnel brinks 135
Seemed in his eye much finer flowers then pinks
& tall wild Woad that lifts its spirey tops
By stone pits — nay een briony & hops
He would from hedges in a poesy bind
& leave the wood bine & the rose behind 140
All wondered at his ways & some believed
The man was crazed but rumour gets decieved
When busy harvest to its end had come
& childern ran to hollow "harvest home"
Bawling half hidden neath each green ash bough 145
For cross plumb shittles out of fashion now
Kate was the queen upon that merry night
& rode upon the waggon drest in white
The stranger oft looked up to see her stand
& smiling called her "queen of fairey land" 150

That harvest supper we had morts of fun
& Farmer Sparks was there a neighours son
He was her fathers choice who dreamed of gain
& talked of marriage as he would of grain
He vainly tryed young Kittys smiles to share 155
& next her without bidding took his chair
Full oft with gracious simperings looking up
To drink to Kitty oer the silver cup
While she but with a careless look replied
Or turned like one that would not heed aside 160
But if the stranger gazed above his horn
She smiled as lovely as a may day morn
Soon as the racket & the fun began
Young Farmer Sparks up from the table ran
To act the crane & poked the room about 165
Breaking the pipes & putting candles out
While wenches squealed & old dames fainted pale
Quickly recovering with an horn of ale
The stranger seemed to shun the rude uproar
& Kate slove with him to the kitchen door 170
I sat on thorns the live long night about
For fear their ways would blab the secret out
& had aught met the fathers jealous sight
Farewell to fun & frolic for the night
But all went right & naught was seen or done 175
To spoil the acting or to damp the fun
The old man smoked his pipe & drank his ale
& laughed most hearty at each sport & tale
On the next day for Kate a gloomy day
The harvest labourers took their parting pay 180
& the young stranger with a downcast eye
Turned round to Kate & bade us both "good bye"
Soon as he went she ran with eager feet
Up stairs to see him vanish down the street
I heard the creeking casement open thrown 185
& knew full well what she neer cared to own
For her swelled eyes their secrets badly kept
When she came down they told me she had wept

Twas harmless sorrows did her bosom move
& theres no sin nor shame to weep for love 190
Sometimes she seemed as sad & sometimes gay
But never more appeared so fond of play
Lone pastimes now did leisure hours engage
Dull as a tamed bird wonted to the cage
She seemed to be while time unheeding went 195
Nor left a hope to ease her discontent
At length the post man with his wind pluft cheek
That brought the news & letters once a week
Some mornings after valentine was bye
Came in & gan his parcel to untie 200
Her sisters bustled up & smiling thought
That he some lovers valentines had brought
But hopes with them was quickly out of date
Soon as they found the letter was for Kate
Poor wench her colour came & went away 205
Now red as crimson then as pale as may
The old man thought it farmer Sparkes's son
That sent the thing & felt his wishes won
Laying his pipe down he began to joke
& clapt her on the shoulder as he spoke 210
Have at him wench thats all I have to tell
& bonny Kate will sell her beauty well
For he's got money wench as well as love
To make your ring sit easy as a glove
But when he found the post mark & the seal 215
Did different notions to his own reveal
He let the mystery undisturbed remain
& turned his chair & took his pipe again
Her sisters bit their lips in silent spite
& could not keep their envye out of sight 220
To think that bonny Kate above them all
Who never in her life had seen a ball
Nor spent an hour to curl her parted hair
Nor of her beauty seemed to have one care
That romped about in play & joined in toil 225
While they would sit & not a finger soil

Should be thus noticed — but they urged a doubt
& muttered some low bred ingenious lout
Had sent the thing & said with louder voice
"Be who he will he wears a vulgar choice" 230
& tho they might clowns valentines condemn
Een they were welcome when they came to them
For Sawney Sparks & each young farmer guest
Was little better then a clown at best
Be who he might it made their bosoms ache 235
& worse when time unriddled their mistake
 Kate had no pride about her she was free
As any maiden in the world could be
& while her sisters dressed in muslin gowns
& scorned on holidays to talk with clowns 240
She seemed to wear no better dress then I
Yet won a look from every passer bye
& some that passed would mutter praises loud
"Theres a sweet face" which never made her proud
She made all equals — used een beggars well 245
& all of Kate had some kind things to tell
 When summer eves the first come swallows meet
As Kate & I were looking down the street
These little summer visitors to view
Marking how lowley & how swift they flew 250
We heard the bustle of a coach & four
Race the lane dust & hurry towards the door
The yard dog never barked nor made a fuss
But dropt his tail & stopt to gaze at us
Een the old geese were silent at the sight 255
& in amazement half forgot their spite
The noisey childern in the street at play
Picked up their tops & taws & sneaked away
& Kate half startled blushed & hurried in
While wonder heaved her bosom to her chin 260
& well it might for twas the very same
Man that at harvest as a reaper came
The same that sent her at the valentine
The clever letter that was wrote so fine

Old women that had muttered round the town 265
& called the stranger by worse names than clown
Peeper out & dropped their courtseys to the coach
& mixed in groups to question its approach
Fine as he was soon as he came in view
I knew his face & so did Kitty too 270
Who over came turned white as was the wall
& almost fainted but he stopt the fall
& kept her in his arms with fondling pain
Till the fresh rose came to her face again
Her father gaped & wondered at the throng 275
& bowed & chattered wether right or wrong
Guessing that love was what the stranger meant
The coach was plenty to buy his consent
& thinking Kate had made her fortune now
He bustled up & gan to scrape & bow 280
& bade Kate welcome in her noble guest
With wine & ale the oldest & the best
But he was not to be by flattery fed
He only smiled & never turned his head
I want no formal welcomes keep your place 285
Old man he said — but why that blushing face
My bonny Kate I left thee fond & true
& wish to find thee as I used to do
Smiling & free as on each harvest morn
When I as labourer reaped thy fathers corn 290
I travelled in disguise alone to find
The native undisguise of womans mind
Theyre easy coyed to take a golden bait
& love in mockery — but my bonny Kate
I found in thee a heart I wished to prove 295
Who ignorant of wealth was caught by love
Then shrink not if thy heart is still sincere
Nor blush nor startle with confounding fear
To see thy mother at this finery awed
& father bow & christen me "my lord" 300
No honours & no titled names are mine
But all I have plain love & wealth is thine

Tho I have grown above thy fathers toil
In reaping corn & ploughing up the soil
Yet that fond love my Kitty showed to me 305
Was neer a moment from my memory
Thy beauty would bewitch a world with love
& Ive returned thy worth & vows to prove
Ive came as promised for thee many a mile
Then bid me welcome with thy usual smile 310
Reach not sweet Kate the silver cup for me
But bring the horn toil often drank to thee
& thus he said but how can words of mine
Relate a speech that he told oer so fine
However there they sat the night about 315
& drank the old brown pitcher nearly out
Kate often smiled but yet was still & shoy
& the old man got down right drunk for joy
Who often reached across his elbow chair
To gain the whisper of his daughters ear 320
Muttering when ere the stranger turned his head
His urgent wishes in her looks to wed
Fingers in vain were shook to keep him still
He een got wilder in his head strong will
"— A good receipt neer makes a bargain wrong 325
"So Kate says he burn nothing with your tongue"
& drank her health anew — the strangers eye
Looked smiling at him but made no reply
When morning came Kate gave her hearts consent
The coach was ordered & to church they went 330
Before the sun the old man bustled up
& gave his blessing oer the silver cup
At the glad closing of that happy day
The stranger drove his blooming bride away
She left her presents for the cake & tea 335
Leaving old gossips in the highest glee
While he with gifts the ringers did regale
Who rung his praises both with bells & ale
& tho she promised me a handsome gown
When eer she married be he gent or clown 340

No wonder that her memorys were away
I quite excused her breaking it that day
    He was no lord tho he was full as great
A country squire with a vast estate
In the most trifling things she had her ends   345
& ere shed gone a twelvemonth from her friends
She wished once more to see us all again
& as indulgence to her lonely pain
They in their coach & four came shining down
To rent a dwelling near her native town   350
& Oakley hall that tops old cromwells hill
He took to please & occupys it still
A fine old place with ivy round the porch
That long had stood as empty as a church
Folks say it is a Cromwells castle been   355
& in the walls still cannon holes are seen
There they in happiness & luxury live
& share the all lifes pleasures has to give
Sometimes they visit at their own estate
& yearly drive to London with the great   360
Whenever I have errands from the town
To seek the hall she gives me many a crown
Making me welcome in plain friendly ways
& often laughs about our younger days
"Hark thats the clock well I must up & roam   365
My man no doubt sits waiting me at home
Wholl scold & say by sitting here till nine
That Im an old fool keeping Valentine
So good night all" & hastening from her seat
She sought her clogs & clocked adown the street   370
The girls were glad twas done — & in her place
The happy cat leapt up & cleaned her face
While crickets that had been unheard so long
Seemed as she stopt to start a merrier song

The Sorrows of Love or The Broken Heart

A Tale

"Good shepherd tell this youth what tis to love
"It is to be all made of sighs & tears —
"————All made of faith & service
"All made of passion & all made of wishes
"All humbleness all patience & impatience
Shakspear [*As You Like It* 5.2.76-7, 82, 88-90]

To sober wi sad truths the laughing mirth
Of rosey daughters round the cottage hearth
Who in the innosence that youth beguiles
Haild new years eve like holidays wi smiles
& pass the winters lengthend eve away 5
A mother told the tale of sally Grey
"How time" she said "& pleasure passes bye"
& stopt to whipe the tear drops from her eye
"Twenty or thirty years when past away
"Seem like an hour glass turnings for one day 10
"Nay fifty years to come the same when gone
"Lives in our memorys scarce the length of one
"Ere half a bottom from the spool is wound
"Or falling water soaketh in the ground
"Time gains upon us distance unawares 15
"Stealing our joys & changing them for cares
"Tis nine & thirty years this very day
"Since I beheld the last of Sally Grey"
Then pausd & lookd above her were she sat
& reachd the bible down to prove the date 20
Whose blank leaves did a catalogue display
Of names & dates the year & month & day
When boys & girls were born & old friends dyd
These still existed memorys certain guide
That lay wi penny storys rustling near 25
& almanacks prese[r]vd for many a year
Stopping the story till she found the place

Pulling her glasses from their leathern case
Twas right & from her lap in saddend vein
She took her knitting & went on again 30
"Poor thing she dyd heart broken & distrest
"Thro love tho docters who may know the best
"Said twas decline that wasted life away
"But truth is truth & be it as it may
"She neer did aught that malice can reprove 35
"Her only failing was the fault of love
"Tis hard enough when innoscen[c]e is hurld
"On the cold bosom of an heartless world
"When mockery & stony hearted pride
"Reveals the failings pity strives to hide 40
"& wi sad cruel taunt & bitter jest
"Lays thorns to pillow troubles broken rest
"But when a poor young thing like Sally dies
"For love & only love were is the eyes
"Can look in memorys face wi out a tear 45
"Een scorn finds nought to turn aside & sneer
"But silent stands while pity shakes her head
"& thinks tears just it self declines to shed
"Twas by anothers failings that she fell
"Whose wanton follys was her passing bell 50
"A clown as wild as young colts freed from plough
"Who saw a prison in a marriage vow
"Had won her heart & kept it in his power
"As the rude bindweed clasps the tender flower
"A clown as shifty as the summer wind 55
"To him her heart & love was all resignd
"Poor girl I felt in trouble for her end
"A next door neighbour & an only friend
"Seldom apart till strangers woud consent
"To take us sisters weresoere we went 60
"Her father kept a cottage next to ours
"A market gardener & he dealt in flowers
"Were swains on sabbath days would oft resort
"To buy fine poesys for a sunday coat

"The 'touchmenot' that like a nettle stung 65
"What ere it met was often hid among
"The flowers of those who lovd rude jokes to trye
"Wi fond unthinking wenches passing bye
"Offering wi serious face as all were well
"Which bit their noses when they bent to smell 70
"& cloves he had the sweetest flower that grows
"& anemonys double as the rose
"Wi velvet 'raculas bepowderd flower
"That lookd as some one in an idle hour
"Had stoopt adown to dust em oer wi meal 75
"& scores of names besides — here oft woud steal
"Poor sallys beau who bought his flowers the while
"Wi double prices money & a smile
"& many a wisper of loves cheating powers
"That calld her fairest of her fathers flowers 80
"Such ways like spring hopes youngling blood did move
"& bye & bye got ripend into love
"He then the wishes of his mind exprest
"& was recievd a lovers welcome guest
"Go were we woud him we was sure to meet 85
"Or on the pasture or about the street
"& oft on summer eves or sabbath days
"Hed join our walks & surfiet her wi praise
"Nay she coud scarcly to the church repair
"But he held out his arm to lead her there 90
"& to her fathers house he often went
"Who welcome gave & deemd it kindly meant
"& crackt of goods & savings oer his ale
"Things he had addld by his spade & flail
"& showing oft wi fatherly regard 95
"The pigs & poultry in his little yard
"How this & that as matters closer led
"Were marriage portions when their daughter wed
"The childern they her little sisters three
"Began to know him & woud climb his knee 100
"& whisperd little storys in his ear

"& calld him brother which he smild to hear
"& to reward them for each prattling way
"He promisd bride cake on the wedding day
"& wi loves keep sakes brought from fair or wake 105
"He near forgot the childerns nutts or cake
"I markd these things for I was often bye
"& ever thought the wedding day was nigh
"For as a neeghbour oft by night & day
"I took my work in to pass time away 110
"& oft wi out it on a winters eve
"Ive stole away nor askd a mothers leave
"To play at cards & talk of dress beside
"For wenches heads are ever after pride
"No holiday ere came but he was there 115
"For whom the father left his corner chair
"Her mother blessd 'em as she touchd the glass
"& wishd him luck & nodded to the lass
"& all beheld him when the freak begun
"In kindred prospect as a promisd son 120
"Thus for awhile his fawning love did burn
"& doubts arose at every touch & turn
"If she but nodded at a fair or wake
"To chaps she knew it made his bosom ache
"Or said 'good morning' to a passer bye 125
"She always had a rival in her eye
"& jealousy woud fawningly complain
"& urge to vows ere he was right again
"But when he found her heart was all his own
"He quickly made his foolish follys known 130
"& like a young bird childern use in play
"He teazd & plagud it till it pind away
"He lovd her on but thought it mighty fun
"To prove her fondness when the maid was won
"From every night to once a week they met 135
"& then excuses made it longer yet
"Somtimes he coud not stay as heretofore
"But calld her out to wisper at the door

"& turnd away & smild self satisfied
"To see the tear drops which she strove to hide 140
"He dancd wi other girls his pride to please
"& seemd to glory in the chance to teaze
"Thinking it fine so many hearts to win
"& smild to see the blushes she was in
"He did such things he said her love to tell 145
"& crackd of morts that lovd him full as well
"At feast & fair Ive seen the fellow start
"Up from his chair to offer girls the quart
"& then look round him wi a leering eye
"& drank their healths while she was sitting bye 150
"Her face burnt red as any cloak the while
"& tears woud startle while she strove to smile
"& oft when nigh a soldier he has sat
"Hed laugh & put the colors on his hat
"But he too great a coward was to go 155
"For nought but cowards uses women so
"Twas only to perplex the heart hed won
"For no one cause but insolence & fun
"& he did hurt her tho she lovd him still
"& patiently put up wi every ill 160
"Nursing the venom of that speckld snake
"About her heart till it was glad to break
"Yet when I cautiond her of loves distress
"& bade her notice the wild fellow less
"Saying she showd her love too much by half 165
" 'Mary you jest' she said & made a laugh
"For we on sabbath days in pleasant weather
"Went still to walk & talk of love together
"& often sought a hut beside the wood
"That from the town a gossips minute stood 170
"Twas calld the herdsmans hut for when her spouse
"Walkd wi out sticks he kept the village cows
"Ere vile enclosure took away the moor
"& farmers built a workhouse for the poor
"Here the old woman for wants small rewards 175

"Woud tell our fortunes both by cups & cards
"Some calld her witch & wisperd all they dare
"Of nightly things that had been noticd there
"Witches of every shape that usd to meet
"To count the stars or mutterd charms repeat 180
"Woodmen in winter as they passd the road
"Have vowd theyve seen some crawling like a toad
"& some like owlets wewing over head
"Shrieking enough to frighten them to dead
"Nay some have witnessd as they passd that way 185
"Grey owlets whooping in the very day
"& in the trees that did their shadows fling
"Close to the door the noisey crows in spring
"Woud build their nests unscard when she was bye
"& tho they saw her never card to flye 190
"& some like kites high overhead woud watch
"Tho shed no chickens in her yard to catch
"Yet she to us appeard like other folks
"A droll old woman full of tales & jokes
"& many a summers eve weve stole away 195
"From bawling cows that needed us to stay
"& neathe the crooked hedge beside the lane
"Oft hid our milk pails till we turnd again
"Were briar & woodbine in the sumer hours
"Hung like a garden coverd oer wi flowers 200
"& soon as ere our shadows reachd the wall
"A magpie which she kept woud scold & bawl
"& peep & follow as we opd the door
"& woud unbidden run its gabble oer
"While she would twirl the tea grounds round the cup 205
"Or take the pack to cut or shuffle up
"Twoud mock the old dame in her deep discourse
"& sqawl so deafning till it een was hoarse
"Till the old dame to let her tale be heard
"Was forcd to take & throw her in the yard 210
"& some woud call & vouchd the thing as true
"The bird a witch that told her all she knew

"I cannot say as what the thing might be
"Twas like the magpies which we always see
"But I am certain wether bad or good 215
"Twoud talk as plain as any christian coud
"Her very cat too bore an evil name
"Because twas fondld up & made so tame
"That like a dog twoud follow her to town
"Purring behind or rubbing by her gown 220
"& oft as homward wi our milk weve came
"Loitering along when chance has met the dame
"Her cat was ever partner in her walk
"& when weve sat the buckets down to talk
"Soon as our eyes was turnd twoud instant plop 225
"To lap the milk upon the bucket top
"& knowing what theyve said about the town
"Ive seen it oft nor card to turn it down
"But if the old dames ways was darkly meant
"I near saw nothing tho I often went 230
"Deal as she might wi satans evil powers
"She read her bible & was fond of flowers
"& went to church as other people may
"& knelt & prayd tho witches cannot pray
"She had her ague charms & old reciepts 235
"For wounds & bruises labour often meets
"& gatherd wild flowers in her summer toils
"To make her ointments that was famd for miles
"& many a one hath ownd her homly skill
"That dare not run a docters larger bill 240
"& as to ill got knowledge of the sky
"She was as innocent as you & I
"She might no doubt wi pointed finger show
"The shepherds lamp which even childer know
"& doubtless lovd when journeying from the town 245
"To see it rising soon as day was down
"The taylors yardband too hung streaming high
"& dicks night waggon driving thro the sky
"& butchers cleaver or the seven stars

"Wi shooting north lights tokening bloody wars 250
"She might know these which if its sin to know
"Then every body is a witch below
"Well those are good that never do no wrong
"& blest are they that scape an evil tongue
"Thus to young hopes she woud her fortunes tell 255
"But sally quickly knew her own too well
"Time by degrees unriddled the mistake
"& left her dreams of fondness wide awake
"Her tears & sighs did all too vainly prove
"To keep the shepherd to his vows of love 260
"He came to vex her oft & woud not stay
"& shut the door agen & laughd away
"Cause she was spotless & a maiden still
"Consience near prickt him that the deed was ill
"& he made promises to give her pain 265
"Just for the sake of breaking them again
"On winter nights for hours Ive known her stand
"Listning wi door half open in her hand
"They say love feels no cold but she has stood
"To wait his coming when he said he woud 270
"Till her very teeth hath chatterd in her head
"Like the third ague ere she went to bed
"So what wi colds & an uneasy mind
"Beauty soon faded & her health declind
"The rose that lovers call so left her face 275
"& the pale sickly lily took its place
"Thus she went on poor mellancholy thing
"Just like a bud thats injurd in the spring
"That may live on to see the coming may
"A feeble blossom leaning on decay 280
"As little linnets pine in summers joys
"For absent loves a shooting clown destroys
"She sorrowd on & worse & worse she grew
"Till strength declind its labour to pursue
"Yet wishing still her sorrows to conseal 285
"She turnd wi feeble hand her spinning wheel

"Till weak & weary when no one was bye
"Shed lean her back ward in her chair to cry
"At length the parents tho wi added fears
"Saw thro her heart throbs & her secret tears 290
"& when they found the only crime was love
"They jokd at times & woud by turns reprove
"Saying if that was all the world possest
"For causing troubles few woud be distrest
"Nor make a grief of such a foolish thing 295
"Were loves were plenty as the flowers in spring
"But all was vain she put her best looks on
"When they was there & grievd when they were gone
"Till toil & fretting brought her down so low
"That she was forcd her labour to forgo 300
"Her friends no longer wi false hopes beguild
"Feard for the danger of their troubld child
"& on the fellows folly closd their door
"& bade him teaze her wi his lies no more
"I often went & sat me by her side 305
"To cheer her spirits while her mother cried
"Who bade her daughter oer & oer agen
"Think more of god & less of naughty men
"But all was vain she made us no reply
"Or only answerd wi a smotherd sigh 310
"Her childern sisters oft hung round her chair
"On which she leant in silence & despair
"Her troubld looks they coud not understand
"& tryd to raise her head from off her hand
"& askd the reason why she sat so still 315
"Or if aught wrongd her that had made her ill
"She kissd their prattling lips wi struggling sighs
"While anguish rushd for freedom to her eyes
"Then woud she turn away from friends & kin
"& hide the trouble that her heart was in 320
"Still woud they teaze her on poor little things
"Twitch at her gown & pull her apron strings
"& eke her sorrow wi her lovers name

"Urging the reason why he never came
"Bringing up childish memorys to her cost 325
"Things they had missd & pleasures she had lost
"Talking of fairings which he usd to bring
"& showing fragments of each broken thing
"Clay sergants broken armd wi faded sash
"& one eyd dolls & churns wi out a dash 330
"Things he oft brought his early suit to move
"Trifles for childern valud proofs for love
"Thus they woud urge & end wi scornfull brow
" 'A naughty man he brings us nothing now'
"She stopt their mouths wi kisses & wi sighs 335
"& turnd her face again to hide her eyes
"Her mother talkd of patience all in vain
"& read jobs troubles oer & oer again
"Then turnd to love & read the book of ruth
"Making excuses for the faults of youth 340
"Saying how she in lifes young joys was crost
"& both a lover & a husband lost
"Yet still hopd on & overlookd the past
"& lovd her mother & was blest at last
"& if said she you trust in god & pray 345
"You may be happy in the end as they
"& she herself woud often try to read
"The bibles comforts in the hour of need
"But soon she faild the cheering truths to look
"& got so weak as scarce to lift the book 350
"The fellow bye & bye his folly mournd
"His consience prickt him or his love returnd
"He begd & prayd & wishd again to be
"Once more admitted to her company
"The parents thought twoud save their sinking child 355
"For troubles hopes are easy reconsild
"& gave the villain leave agen to come
"& more then that to make their cot his home
"When he came first I sat beside her bed
"He askd her how she was & hung his head 360

"She bursted into tears & coud not speak
"& as she leand her sorrow wasted cheek
"Upon her hand he did his sins recall
"She kissd him fondly & forgave him all
"Her face was thin & lost its healthy red 365
"White as the sheets turnd down upon her bed
"No doubt he felt an anguish in her pain
"& seemd to pause ere he coud speak again
"Vows he renewd as cures for every ill
"She turnd to me & sighd 'they never will' 370
"Then smild & bowd her faded face to weep
"& wearied out sunk down like one asleep
"Then rose agen like one awoke from pain
"& gazd on him & me & wept again
"& on her bosom laid her wasted hand 375
"Sighing a language b[r]utes might understand
"He took her hand but the poor mother prayd
"His stay to comfort the dejected maid
"He heard it gladly & he did remain
"Set down his stick & closd the door again 380
"& of their humble living shard a part
"& livd an inmate of her house & heart
"& hopes was fed tho but the mask of pain
"As she recoverd & got out again
"She seemd so well they een began to name 385
"The wedding day — twas set & ere it came
"Hope got so strong her friends were fixd upon
"To act as bride maids & myself was one
"While gossips when they met woud still agree
"To shake their heads & say twoud never be 390
"Muttering oer doubts they woud not urge aloud
"Saying her bride dress woud turn out a shroud
"God knows they but too truly prophesyd
"For ere it came she sickend worse & dyd
"Upon that very morn that was to be 395
"The wedding sunshine & festivity
"Death did so gently his cold fingers lay

"Upon her bosom that she sild away
"Without a groan & but for us that wept
"About her bed one might have thought she slept 400
"For marriage greetings parents sorrows fell
"& marriage peals changd to a passing bell
"Her young sun set neath sorrows settld cloud
"Wed to the grave her bride sheets was a shroud
"& I who thought to see her dress that day 405
"A brides wi love notts dizend out so gay
"Saw it preparing at the joiners shop
"Who trimd the white lace round the coffin top
"They usd to use it in my early day
"For such as went off young like sally grey 410
"He was a merry man & always free
"& stopt his work to throw a nail at me
"There Mary take you that he smild & said
"Twill help for yours in case you die a maid
"I passd it off for jokings mean no ill 415
"& I have kept it for her memory still
"Aye aye instead of joining in the throng
"Of merry faces & a wedding song
"Instead of seeing her a bride become
"I bore the pall up to her last long home 420
"& heard the old clerks mellancholy stave
"That sung the psalm bareheaded by her grave
"Life to a spiders web had wore & spun
"& een her hands if lifted to the sun
"Were both so wasted that to fancys view 425
"The light woud almost seem to glimer thro
  "Thus dyd poor sally on her wedding day
"An april bud that could not see the may
"Nor did the cause from whence her cares begun
"Live long to mourn the evil he had done 430
"A year scarce past—god every evil sees
"Ere he was struck wi sickness & disease
"The small pox came that blight to girls & boys
"& spreading famine of a mothers joys

"Waking its fears of danger far & wide 435
"But none save him throughout the village dyd
"Poor sallys parents who forgave the wrong
"Agreed to his last wishes right or wrong
"& close beside the church yards gravel way
"He lyes a schoolboys leap from sally grey 440
"I often stood to gaze upon the stone
"When ere I journeyd to the church alone
"Were gold wingd cherubs held a flowery wreath
"Over a prayer book open underneath
"Upon whose leaves was writ at her request 445
"In gilded letters 'here the weary rest'
"Last spring one sabbath day I loiterd there
"Before the bells had chimd the hour of prayer
"Stopping as pity seemly did demand
"I wrapt my apron corner round my hand 450
"& pulld the nettles that had overgrown
"The verse & rambld half way up the stone
"My tale is growing fast but I must tell
"What in my mind will [n]ever cease to dwell
"Some people make a mock & laugh at dreams 455
"& call them shades were things so plainly seems
"& say tis silly as a maid to stand
"& let the gipsey cross her in the hand
"Well let folks laugh I think it not so well
"Wi joking ways on serious things to dwell 460
"I think dreams truths myself or mostly such
"& joseph in the bible thought as much
"Nay he the causes of such visions knew
"& pharoahs baker found his words too true
"All eyes may see it if they do but look 465
"Then who woud laugh & disbelieve the book
"The dream I have to tell which sally told
"Woud make ones flesh in dog days creep wi cold
"& as to proofs I think it needeth none
"Truth proves itself so listen till Ive done 470
"Once in our lives when follys did decieve

"We made the dumb cake upon saint marks eve
"Sitting on thorns we scarcly dare to wait
"Ere twas half done we took it off the slate
"& walking backwards up the stairs to bed 475
"We thought one followd wi a sliving tread
"& sally startling faster wi the fright
"Burnt her loose capstring as she held the light
"She shriekd to see it & we spoild the cake
"For when folks do it nones alowd to spake 480
"Had we been still plain shadows of the men
"That were to court us woud have risen then
"But sally spoke & we no further knew
"Of what Ive heard old women vouch as true
"& sure I am we heard the stepping sound 485
"Of somthing stealing lightly oer the ground
"As one at 'I spy' sliveth gently on
"They seemd as wishing to approach unknown
"Just like cats stepping upon boarden floors
"But none were there wed turnd em out of doors 490
"We hastend into bed to fears repose
"& hid our faces underneath the cloaths
"Nor dare we stay to put the candle out
"But left it burning half the night about
"& dare not once unclose a waken eye 495
"Lest aught shoud come & push the curtains bye
"For we as was agreed wi parents leave
"Slept both together on that witches eve
"But I saw nothing worser then myself
"& heard what might be mice upon the shelf 500
"Tho sally dreamd & when she told it me
"Quakd like a winter leaf upon the tree
"& many a day it made her memory ach
"For she still fancyd she was wide awake
"She thought her lover came beside her bed 505
"& lookd in trouble & hung down his head
"& shook her hand & wi a heavy smile
"From out his pocket took a ring the while

"Twoud fit no finger tho he tryd em all
"& dropt & broke to ashes in the fall 510
"& instantly she said she seemd to see
"Herself as plain as you appear to me
"Bend by his side as one thats weak & sick
"& aids the loss of strength upon a stick
"Wi face all pale & nought but skin & bone 515
"& yet she felt that it was like her own
"She vowd she saw them at the alter stand
"Plain as I see this knitting in my hand
"Both in a long dress wrapt from head to feet
"Like shadows folks in haunted places meet 520
"Molds seemd she said the alter steps to pave
"Mingld wi terrors like a new made grave
"Rust eaten nails & bones in pieces cleft
"By sextons spades & tarnishd letters left
"On breastplates which once buried names had spelt 525
"She saw all these & frighted as she felt
"She coud not wake & were the green cloth lay
"On th' alters table every sabbath day
"A black one hung & in full folds did wreath
"As if it hid a coffin underneath 530
"The bells seemd knolling too a heavy sound
"Like pots thats crackt or somthing under ground
"Or as the clock the hour in winter tells
"Muffld in snow they humd like passing bells
"She shriekd & woke me but she dare not name 535
"The cause of terror till the daylight came
"She often feard its end & were alas
"Has dismal dreams brought sadder proofs to pass
"I thought dreams truths let folks laugh as they will
"& if tis foolish I believe em still 540
"Last christmass eve when ye were at the door
"Whispering wi sweethearts your love secrets oer
"I took my glasses to amuse myself
"& reachd the bible down from off the shelf
"To read the text & look the psalms among 545

"To find the one that at her grave was sung
"The place had long been doubld down before
"& much I wishd ye in to read it oer
"Your fathers read it to me many a time
"When ye were young & on our laps woud climb 550
"Nay keep your work tis not worth while to leave
"Ill sit & hear it on to morrow eve
"For even if the night woud time alow
"My hearts so sad I cannot hear it now
"Ive talkd till I have almost tird my tongue 555
"Folks say old womens tales are always long
"So here Ill end & like it as ye may
"I wish ye better luck then sally grey"
She ceasd her tale & snuffd the candle wick
Lifting it up from burning in the stick 560
That soon had faild to light her story out
Had she continued spinning it about
Then laid her knitting down & shook her head
& stoopd to stir the fire & talk of bed

The Rivals

A Pastoral

Beneath a meadow brig whose arch was dry
Some shepherds gatherd till a shower was bye
Upon whose smooth half circling roof of stone
Rude figurd scrawls in different colors shone
Spread hands & birds & self imagind flowers 5
Pastimes of hinds imprisond there by showers
Some made wi ruddle that the shepherd swain
Uses to mark & know his sheep again
& some by firesticks chances haply find
About the spot by gipseys left behind 10
& many a deeply cut two letter name
Were knives was spoilt to win an inch of fame
That linger on for years about the spot
Brands of oblivion living yet forgot
There the swains lingerd till the storm was oer 15
Sitting on stones rolld in for seats before
Some sat them down at leisures pleasant toil
& made them apple scopes of bone the while
One crimpt a nitting skeath upon his knees
To please a maiden whom he wishd to please 20
An older swain did his wet rest employ
In making whistles for an anxious boy
Who sat in anxious watchings by his side
Waiting their finish with exulting pride
While two young swains in loves discoursings fell 25
Lapping up love knott platts & many a spell
Of broad green reed blades were the sheltered midge
Dancd in their shadows by the mossy bridge
Swallows that darted thro the arch at play
Heard the rude noise & popt another way 30

Richard

My love forgets me never every spell
Links as I lap it & betokens well

When I was young & went a weeding wheat
We usd to make them on our dinner seat
& laid two blades across & lapd them round 35
Thinking of those we lovd & if we found
Them linkd together when unlapt again
Our love was true if not the wish was vain
An old droll woman who first told it me
Vowd that a truer token coud not be 40

Simon

Three times Ive lapd mine up & still tis out
A fatal number had I cause to doubt
But Mary field flower still is fond & free
& near shows nothing to dishearten me
I care not what such foolish trifles tells 45
For I can bring up better proofs then spell[s]

Richard

Then show them Simon for if she be true
To lovers vows she has no room for two
Near feast on fancy tis a dangerous food
To take as earnest in a loving mood 50
She throws a rosey veil round self conse[i]t
That like the canker round the heart will eat
Till theres ought left to cherish her disguise
Then like worm eaten fruit it drops & dies
If I judge right the maid you name is mine 55
Nor without proofs will I her truth resign

Simon

These I can give in plenty tho I own
I never knew that she had kindness shown
To other shepherds then my self till now
& much more chaind her freedom with a vow 60
Last old may fair when I got bold wi beer
I lovd her long before but had a fear
To speak as by a stall she chancd to stand
Wi kerchief full of farings in her hand

I venturd up & tapd her oer the arm 65
She seemd at first to startle wi alarm
But when I begd a faring at the wake
She loosd her kerchief & pulld out a cake
& in return for her good naturd ways
I offerd ribbons which I heard her praise 70
But she refusd & said shed plenty got
& thankd me kindly tho she had them not

Richard

When ere at sunday feast or rushing fair
I go & meet wi rosey Mary there
If my dog finds her first he rubs her cloaths 75
& wags his tail een she to him bestows
A ginger button & quick turns agen
Thinking his masters not far from her then
& when she notices were I may be
She comes unaskd to offer things to me 80
& neer refuses the returns I make
But meanest trifles condesends to take
& when Im backward in my gifts to try
Her love shell ask me what I mean to buy
Last christmas blast I joind the skaiting crew 85
That yearly racd for hats wi ribbons blue
& swam away wi young hopes swiftest pace
Nor was I cheated for I won the race
& when I took the ribbons home at night
To Mary she seemd trembling wi delight 90
& near refusd the profferd gift to take
But said well done Ill keep it for your sake

Simon

Once we with others at a neighbours met
To play at cards when she agen me set
& tho at first she edgd her chair away 95
She got more free as we began to play
& from the table as my cards I took
Shed smile & oer my shoulder steal a look

To make believe in true loves fondling way
She wishd to know the cards I had to play 100
& when to try her love I made pretence
To leave off playing for the wants of pence
She from her lap took out the penny fee
& put it neath the candlestick for me
& tho she woud not take when we retird 105
My hand to guide her home as I desird
She said tho night was dark the way was short
& wishd good night & thankd me kindly fort

Richard

Last martinmass at night we joind to play
A hand or two & keep a holiday 110
When we chusd partners not as love regards
But by the fortunes of the lifted cards
When Mary peept at one she took in hand
& lookd at me to make me understand
Pointing the color in her flowery dress 115
I took the hint & well knew which to guess
The colord card said I my guesses seek
Is somthing like the rose on marys cheek
A bonny red for me — she laughd outright
& said then Im your partner for the night 120
& blushd & hitchd her chair up close to mine
& paid wi joy her kiss for every fine
When the hour came for mirth & time to part
Tho it was late she seemd as loath to start
& tho the full moon shone as bright as day 125
She almost askd me if Id lead the way
Making broad signs by many an urgd complaint
How she had sat till she was fit to faint
& the rude cumbering umberella got
To load her journey when twas wanted not 130
I took the hint & askd if she woud go
When she jumpd up wi out the least ado
& took my arm nor illness longer feignd
& quite fo[r]got that she had ere complaind

These are plain proofs & I can bring up morts 135
To show whose name is nearest in her thoughts

Simon

Once neath a hugh ash tree she made a stop
To view a magpies nest upon the top
I thought she wishd the eggs & up I went
Nor stopt to ask her looking what it meant 140
The grain sweed like a bulrush in the wind
But I clumb on & left my fears behind
She praisd the spotted eggs but seemed in pain
So up I took them to the nest again
Poor birds she sighed to hear them noise & flye 145
Tho more perhaps to think Id clumb so high
I was emboldend from such shown regard
To beg & take a kiss as my reward
& tho behind her hands she hid her face
She only blushd nor frownd at my embrace 150

Richard

Force puts no choice their own free will is best
What we urge earnest they but take in jest
One day while picking sprigs of hillock thyme
A little pismire in the flowers did climb
That to her bosom proved a rebel guest 155
& stung her as she placed it in her breast
Red pimples rose upon the snowy skin
& sighs bespoke the anguish it was in
But when she showed it me with blushing face
I bent with trembling heart & kissed the place 160
Urging the charm as cure for all her pain
She smiled as wishing to be kissed again

Simon

Once in the pasture lane at evenings hours
She stoopd adown to reach the brooks flag flowers
& sure enough had I not caught her gown 165
Headlong the venturing girl had toppld down

& the deep pit where she had nigh fell in
It takes the sunday bathers to the chin
I held her in my arms till dangers fright
Was calmd & then she bade me a good night 170
I woud have kissd her but she said me nay
& smiling promisd as she walkd away
To dance wi me on the next holiday

Richard

Once from her choice black lamb I stoopd to pull
A bramble that got tazzeld in the wool 175
& prickd my hand she seemd to feel the pain
& tryd wi pin to pick it out in vain
& sighs the while did her white bosom swell
& tear drops startld while she wishd it well
Owning she wishd Id let the lambkin be 180
As she had rather it were hurt then me

Simon

Aye some delights to try a gossips spell
& flatterys honey suits some lovers well
Ive took her milk full often oer a stile
She always thankd me & woud often smile 185
& when shes missd a lamb at morns young light
Thinking the fox had stole it off at night
Shed mourn & sigh & seek it & enquire
When I searchd too oft prickd wi thorn & briar
& when she sorrowd tho the lamb was free 190
I might think to[o] that she was grievd for me

Richard

Thoughts deals in fancys far away from truth
& follys shadows shine like suns to youth
But reasons proofs are never urgd in vain
& what Ive witnessed Ill believe again 195
Once neath this very bridge when left alone
I cut my name in full upon the stone
Twas weeding time & she was toiling nigh

Wi others cutting thistles from the rye
& one day coming to the place again 200
When they had been for shelter from the rain
I saw her own name in full letters shine
Scratchd wi a knife or bodkin close to mine
& linkd together wi a trueloves knott
Mine lingers still upon the much lovd spot 205
But some rude fool wi envy at his heart
Has scratchd hers out & tore the links apart
& let them hide loves shadows as they will
The heart that wrote is my possesion still
I told her of the proof wi anxious pride 210
& tho she ownd it not she near denyd

Simon

On plough witch monday I was in the barn
Tying my bottles up of foddering corn
To take afield for sheep that round the stacks
Lay wi the small snow winnowing on their backs 215
When in she came wi cheeks as pale as death
& scarce coud spake the while for want of breath
Keep secrets Sim she said I need them now
The witch chaps come & skulkd behind the mow
& in they brushd & laughd & stird about 220
Threatning rude kisses if they found her out
While I to screen her as she wishd me swore
That I had seen her bustle by the door
So off they ran & she came smiling out
& said she hated to be slaumd about 225
Wi their black faces—but when I began
To urge my claims she never shriekd & ran
As from a snake or toad—but said the day
Was short & labour had no time for play

Richard

But hark ye Simon thats in seasons gone 230
On last plough monday I myself was one
She saw us coming & prepard to flee

But oer her shoulder left a laugh on me
She hid as one that wishes to be found
& while the others lookd the house around 235
I heard the creaking of the dairey door
Knowing such secrets by her ways before
& instant put her hiding place to rout
Nor did she hold the latch to keep me out
She might my grizzld face a little dread 240
"Youll spoil my sunday cap" she cringd & said
I hopd she woud not take my ways unkind
"O no" she laughd "theres water never mind"

Simon

Some sundays back Id been to fold my sheep
Just as the red sun down the woods did creep 245
& looking back while wandering home again
I saw a girl come down the pasture lane
& slackend pace to pull a wild rose down
That she might catch me ere we met the town
& turning round again as near she drew 250
Twas marys self who nodded "how do ye do"
& joind & chatterd freely by my side
Oft turning round my happy dog to chide
Who chasd the hares that sat on clover knolls
At feed & rabbits squatting by their holes 255
& praisd the black bird at his evening song
That in the hedgerow ranted all along
His old song "Draw the knave a cup of beer
"Be quick quick quick" in chorus plain & clear
Such sounds will oft old womens thoughts engage 260
Who mock the tame ones in their wicker cage
At length the crossing field of corn came on
Were the path only spard a room for one
Tho she went first still she woud often turn
The unheard answers of our talk to learn 265
& oft as if she wishd it love the while
Shed ask me what it was I said & smile
Ive oft wishd since Id tryd at ways to woo

& gone before to brush the damping dew
& tho half shoy & fearful all the while 270
I never urgd to help her oer a stile
Shed let me climb them first & make a stand
As if she wishd to offer me her hand
But I kept backward purposly to prove
The self betrayings of my marys love 275
& sure enough all that have eyes may see
Thro this the value that she has for me

Richard

They may indeed & mary in her mirth
Woud say a farthing is of kindred worth
Last may day eve she spraind her foot at play 280
& when she found she coud no longer stay
She came to me & made broad signs the while
To lead her home & help her oer each stile
Some said she feignd it as excuse to go
Be as it woud I near enquird to know 285
But took her arm & went & on our road
She many a smile & many a kiss bestowd
Till I een fancyd tho I said it not
That all was feignd for she her wounds forgot
& as she leand to rest agen a stile 290
The pale moon hanging oer her looks the while
"Richard" she said & laughd "the moon is new
"& I will try if that old tale is true
"Which gossips tell who say that if as soon
"As any one beholds the new may moon 295
"Bright leaning oer green fields of grass & corn
"Slender & crooked like an old rams horn
"They oer their eyes a silken kerchief fling
"That has been slided thro a wedding ring
"As many years as they shall single be 300
"As many moons they thro that blind shall see
"& I for once will try the truth I vow
"For this that hangs about my bosom now
"Was drawn thro one upon a bridal night

"When we was full of gossip & delight 305
"Old women if they knew me dot woud call
"Me fond & think I wishd the number small
"Een you may think me foolish or too free
"But be ast will Ill take it off I see"
Then instant from her moon gilt neck she threw 310
It first oer me & bade me tell her true
& sure as I stand here while that was oer
I saw two moons as plain as one before
"Bless me" she said & when she put it on
She laughd & told me she coud see but one 315
But when I bade her look agen & try
She then saw two the very same as I
& as the kerchief round her neck she tyd
She laughd & said well now Im satisfied
Mary I answerd then it rests wi you 320
To suit the tale & make it false or true
She took my arm & said I[m] glad to find
The new moon proves us both with in a mind
This was as plain a hint as she coud say
& other proofs were throwing words away 325
Yet she made promises that night to me
That next years summer may expect to see
When a love nott between us shall be twind
As fast as rings & parsons words can bind

Simon

Ill not believe it tho I own her ways 330
Much more of freedom then I wishd betrays
Still her good manners I will keep in mind
& near believe that marys so unkind
She always thanks me very kind & free
For help in toil & thats a proof for me 335
Last live long winter thro for such rewards
I cleard the pads from snow about the yards
& litterd straw in all the pudgy sloughs
About the hovel were she milkd her cows
& often milkd when I had time in hand 340

& from the heath brought many a load of sand
When ere at plough or muck-cart I have been
Her shining rows of pewter plates to clean
& oft in summer kept away from church
In stead of her the old hens nests to search 345
& slove up from my supper many a day
When master at the market was away
For her a stolen pear or plumb to reach
Or gait of water from the pump to fetch
& she has smild & thankd me oer & oer 350
Love proves itself I need not tell no more
Yet once while clambering oer the orchard wall
I fell & from my pocket in the fall
My knife was lost — & mary ever free
Found it & offered it as mine to me 355
But I denyd it then that mine was gone
On purpose that the maid might keep it on
So she no more inquirys card to make
& Ill be bound she wishd it for my sake

Richard

Well tho I had not time to tend her so 360
Or milk her cows or clear her pads of snow
Love has no out door charms for winter weather
Twas spring & summer when we met together
Yet when a chance fell out — at her desire
I waited on her at the kitchen fire 365
& often made her evening labour light
& took the hugh pot off the hooks at night
Brim full of milk the cady calves to feed
& soon as chances left no eyes to heed
Were soon as ere she thought the job was oer 370
Shed make excuse to meet me at the door
In whispering ways shed oer my shoulder lean
While I took kisses from my toil unseen
Whenever she sat up to bake or brew
I slove to help her when no body knew 375
While she woud of her own accord agree

To hunt the yard & seek new eggs for me
Seeking about when all were safe abed
Neath cribs & straw wiout a fear or dread
Nor dreaded striding witch or sheated ghost 380
To lap them up in the hot coals to roast
Tho shed no cellar key an horn to fill
I filld a sweet wort dish & sipt at will
Tho she drank none at those late hours of stealth
Shed sip & own it was to drink my health 385
& when the summer blossoms ceasd to bloom
& time to take the honey up was come
When the blue brimstone torch was set alight
To smother in ther hives the bees at night
When she would call it cruelty & sigh 390
& often take her apron up to cry
Yet thought tho troubled oer each murderd bee
To save the whitest honeycomb for me
& oft shed from her folded apron take
Gifts venturing chaps had stolen for her sake 395
& bade me chuse what ere I might prefer
& oft to prove I left the chance to her
When in a minute shed begin to seek
A favourite apple wi the reddest cheek
Or plumb that lookd the mellowest — the while 400
Holding them out wi many a sweeter smile
& if I fetchd her water from the well
Shed slive out too some secret tale to tell
Tho the true cause was hid in loves deciet
She wishd to hear the hour at eve to meet 405
These are not only proofs of love but speak
Things plain as ever one may wish to seek
As to the knife there all your hopes must sink
Know knives cut love not keep it as you think
One that she picked up once you soon may see 410
Such gifts are dangerous so she sold it me
So own it if you can Ill that resign
But Mary Field flower still I claim as mine
Aye Simon lad why turn ye from the view

Play wi your watch chain when youve nought to do 415
Look up & answer me or else refrain
& own youve lost & well be friends again

Aye said the old man wi a sickening smile
Whod shut his knife to listen them awhile
Poor Simons baffld hopes have stood too long 420
His proofs were seldom right & often wrong
His chance is bad I own if all be true
So make it up & have no more to do
Throw down the foolish love ye long have nurst
& done or else the rain will finish first 425
Simon who from their gaze had turnd around
& wi his hook progd holes about the ground
Whistled his rested dog lapt up asleep
& in the rain went seeking up his sheep
Glad from a rivals triumph to retreat 430
Yet near acknowledgd that himself was beat
While Richard turnd his comrades talk to join
& proudly sneerd to see his foe resign

Opening of the Pasture – Love & Flattery

Within a closes nook beneath a shed
Nigh to the stack where stock in winter fed
Where black thorn thickets crowded close behind
& shielded cows & maidens from the wind
Two maidens sat free from the pasture sloughs 5
& told each other as they milked their cows
Their evening thoughts of love — while over head
The little Wren from its new dwelling fled
Who neath the hovels thatch with spring-hopes blest
Began to hang & build its curious nest 10
Of hair & feathers & root mosses green
It watched about & pickt its feathers clean
& cocked its tail & sung its evening strain
Then fluttering ventured to its nest again
While bluecaps blest the swelling buds to see 15
Repeated their two notes from tree to tree
The ass untethered rambling at his ease
Knapt the black budding twigs of ashen trees
& sheep the green grass champt with greedy bite
A certain sign of sudden showers at night 20
The mavis sung aloud & seemed to say
Arise my timid love & come away
Fear not the cold the winters gone & past
& green leaves come to hide our homes at last
The woodman humming takes his homeward track 25
With his night faggot bending at his back
& in his button hole he gladly bears
The firstling primrose that the forrest heirs
To show his wife & childern the glad news
That spring is hastening with her nursing dews 30
& while the fire light in their faces glowers
He tells his forrest tales of birds & flowers
Here sat the maids in health & beauty blest
Talking of love their leisures common guest
The Wren might think them when it tried to sing 35
The two first blossoms of the early spring

But when the pastures melted snow was oer
Daisey[s] were seen some dozen days before

Mary

How sweet the lengthening eve begins to come
The grass gets green & flowers begin to bloom 40
& birds to build their nests — soon suns will dry
The roads that we may set our pattens bye
The chirping birds now feel the winter oer
Nor longer mope about the threshers door
"Pink pink" the bunting says I love the sound 45
It seems to call the daiseys oer the ground
Dear heart I love to see the quiet spring
Come teaching first the little birds to sing
Then loitering in the sunny field & street
Like people telling stories when they meet 50
& often pausing in a showers delay
As if she feared some danger by the way
Sending her herralds forward one by one
To try the journey she herself is on
Now starts a daisy then a buttercup 55
& then a little primrose trembles up
& thus she comes like to a timid maid
Of ruffling winds & dirty roads affraid
& warm light eves when lovers leisure grows
Whole hours to talk & meet in ere they close 60
When Richard will have penned his sheep ere dark
& I shall hear his old dogs happy bark
As from the heaths furze-hill he hastens down
To milk my cows & join me to the town
I dearly love the evenings sober hue 65
That from her hazey garments scatters dew
While night creeps on by stealth & never shows
A track to tell us whence he comes & goes
Love in such partings feel[s] more joy then pain
That hopes next evening hours to meet again 70

Lucy

Well I am sick of plough mens vulgar ways
Teazing ones sunday evenings walk with praise
Their cuckoo-songs of "ducky" "love" & "dear"
So oft repeated sicken me to hear
Three grains of common sense they dont possess 75
& they're such down right hobbies in their dress
A scarlet waist coat is their common wear
Tis ploughmens livery — that I cannot bear
& then a ribbon dangles from his hat
He thinks himself a down right squire with that 80
I hate such tawdry whims & blockhead taste
A gipsey looks much better when hes drest
I cannot bear the dirty loves of clowns
Sullying ones kerchief & ones sunday gowns
Crumpling ones bonnet every now & then 85
To steal a kiss — I hate such clownish men
Theyve no more manners then a colt broke loose
& no more sense then is a silly goose
Bold brazen talk is down right wit with them
& gentry with good manners they condemn 90
They call them evil names & stand & laugh
Like a rude jack ass & a brawling calf
But ask them one plain thing in reasons way
They yawn & cough say "hah" or nothing say
Commend me to a tinker if you will 95
But these clot hoppers I dislike them still

M[ary]

Aye scornful Lucy what has Simon done
That you his love & all his kind should shun
I fear from higher life some dressy beau
Has urged your love to scorn poor Simon so 100
Beware of cox combs wench what says the song
"Theres mischief lurks beneath a flatterers tongue"
A pedlar once ran his door story oer
& spread his wares agen our kitchen door
Young Farmer Folly passing saw the shews 105

& asked if there was aught that I could chuse
Though I chose nought not caring to be free
He stoopt & bought this ivory case for me
He would have bought a broach but none was left
& knife with silver heart upon the heft 110
He took it first then said it would not do
As they would cut the closest love in two
Then paid the gabbering man & laghed away
To every offer I had said him nay
But the poor pedlar seeing me afraid 115
Said honour honest callings pretty maid
Far do I walk & poorly am I paid
& if such rosey cheeks are turned to frown
Upon my calling — I am broken down
So for pedlars sake & not for his 120
I took the gift nor thought the fault amiss
& heres a knitting sheath one carved for me
Out of the brown heart of the damsin tree
Nor would I give it would it buy the place
This simple token for this ivory case 125

L[ucy]

Well I see nothing in the shape of pride
To put good offers when their met aside
The sloe & crab are hedgrows common wear
But plumbs & apples gardens only bear
& if a fortune finding met my eye 130
Who would be fool to pass it you or I

M[ary]

For fortunes gifts folk oft wrong names employ
As every finder meets not fortunes joy
As seeds will vary from the finest tree
So beautys baits will often poison be 135
The haughty maid by gazing on the skies
May miss the love gift that beneath her lies
To turn your back on honesty may show
Worse luck at last then passing an odd crow

Good fortunes ever found on safest ways 140
Danger lays traps — good fortune nothing lays
But honest truth disdaining all disguise
& truth tho poor is still esteemed a prize
To look for luck to rise above ourselves
Is just as vain as if yon man that delves 145
In the wood ditch should look around his toil
To turn up buried money with the soil
Tis infants only that will pule & cry
For flickering stars that spangle in the sky
Some trust to moles & dreams — I think it well 150
To link no hope with every idle spell
For doubt & sorrow are two dangerous weeds
Whose roots strike deep whose flowers shed bitterest seeds
— Look heres a mole hid underneath my gown
Upon my breast — & shall I double down 155
The fortune boook that tells such spots to be
Omens of good or evil unto me
& if it speaks of wealth — wealth may not come
So who'd deck rooms to make such guests a home
Where dissapointments following hopes & fears 160
Is sure to change hopes laughter into tears
For pride is always neighbour to consciet
& ignorance just makes the thing compleat
That looks on beauty as a common toy
Which brings to fancy momentary joy 165
That sees it fade & weary with the view
Sickens & hankers after somthing new
But truth of love will always wear a smile
The coarsest jointure & the hardest toil
Is ever sweet while theres a friend to share 170
The heavy lot thats fallen to our care
But when we stumble on a mirey road
& the staff breaks that should have born the load
Our lot & life is wear[i]some & we
Have the true lot of falsehoods misery 175
— Upon the chimney top wake when I will
The morn-watch swallows are "twit tweeing" still

& if I rise ere morning opes her eye
Theres sure to be a sky lark in the sky
Gay natures always laughing — things may die 180
She never goes in mourning where they lie
Nor true love ever hath a cause for grief
For providence will give to truth relief
Unlooked for troubles often may arise
But greatest griefs will often whipe their eyes 185
& roughest days find out their journeys end
& those most lonely find at last a friend
But dissapointment like a worm in may
Lives on & nothing drives the grief away

L[ucy]

Well smiles that with the sunniest pleasures dwell 190
May often meet with sorrows tears as well
Yet things I like not shant abuse my feet
Ill never run an enemy to meet
Bees often labour in a rainy hour
& gather honey from a poisonous flower 195
Nor in the sunshine of youths fairy dreams
Will I dread shadows where no shadow seems
For if you stand at that — whats happiness
But half way troubles in a different dress
Mere trifling parents of a laugh or smile 200
To cheat our hearts & sooth our hopes awhile
Mere sundays left between a working day
To catch our breath & give us time to play
Most joys beginnings have one tale to tell
Whose common ends an heart ach & farewell 205
The kisses pressed upon mere prudish lips
May be loves bees that for mock honey sips
& emblems oft of the decievers game
& just no more of loving but the name
For oaths like china ware — a brittle token 210
Tho full as fair are just as easy broken
Loves merry sorrows I shall never mind
Tho bees have stings & pain is left behind

Ill like the sunshine smile on every thing
& frown no shadows cause I fear a sting 215
One that is poor mere fortune seldom steals
& bonds are safe that warm affection seals
A narrow oak plank oer a flood washed stream
Looks dismal as a danger in a dream
But if we pass safe oer it — never mind 220
The brig & danger both have acted kind
& if good fortunes mine Ill use it well
& never think Im fallen till Ive fell

M[ary]

Good fortune comes of merit more then wealth
Caution brings both — as medicine brings us health 225
& if we do not look before we leap
We may fall headlong down some dizzy steep
Indeed we may — & rocks were dangers dwell
Lie often pashed to fragments were they fell
To prove a person of inferior kind 230
Is only proving of their want of mind
By looks the gentleman is poorly told
As bad as pinch backs glitter taen for gold
Yet [hide] a clown in gold you hide in vain
His brazen speech the very gold would stain 235
& pride alone what is it but the fop
That stands for somthing when he leaves his shop
Yet of so little value with the great
— They seem as free as your young mistress Kate
— A man on horseback passed me tother night 240
I dropt a courtsey as good manners might
He instant touched his hat & made a bow
Tho I was dressed as plain as I am now
I thought it somthing strange yet nothing knew
Till our old hedger down his faggot threw 245
To ask me if I knew him — no said I
"Why thats his Lordship — aye it is beguy"
I burnt with wonder so I scarce could speak
You might have lit a candle in my cheek

He took me for my mistress then I said 250
Lords would not make such manners to a maid
"Yes yes" said he "how high so ere they be
"He shows good manners even unto me["]
—So now I know however some decide
Real gentlefolks are never made of pride 255
Such pleasant actions better shows a man
Then proud pretending cox comb fooleries can
We often throw a stone to ford a stream
& try with sticks where deeper places seem
—But straws & dust & feathers & such kind 260
Are ever thrown to tell us wheres the wind
& proud young fops I still dislike & shun
& think it rude tho masters joke in fun
"Mary" he'll stand & say "tis somewhat quere
"But in my house theres roseys all the year 265
"How is it wench" he'll ask then stand & stare
—"Look in the glass & you will find them there["]
& thus he would his vain tomfooleries move
& thought I took his poor consciet for love
He would with sneering smile my looks extoll 270
& scold the Parrot when it called me "Poll"
& oft he'll call me from my work at night
To mend his fire & candle fresh to light
—& then he needs me not—& there I stand
Just like a post with door latch in my hand 275
& then he'll do't himself & joke the while
That my fair looks was never made for toil
& says tis pity that so fine a face
Neer met with favours for a better place
I sneak away & blush out right for shame 280
& mutter madness tho I fear to blame
Yet he shall never make my weakness win
Repenting fondness in the arms of sin
The youth tho poor whose memory lives with me
Has got a heart of better worth then he 285
One day he pluckt a rosey from the tree
Saying Mary heres your sister do you see

—I did see compliments had little power
To prove love lasting by a withering flower
& tother night as I sat on the bench 290
Beside the door he said my "rosey wench"
I think you fond of books as well as flowers
So here is one to please your leisure hours
Twas "Bloomfields Poems" they were sweet indeed
He turned a leaf down where he bid me read 295
It was a story called "the broken crutch"
"Theres luck" said he "your face might get as much"
—I loved the poems & the story too
But with the lady I had small to do
I owned no face to stir a poets pen 300
While common praise belongs to common men
& any wench who stops upon her way
May stoop at nothing twenty times a day
Twas not my inclination & desire
To set my cap at farmer Gent or Squire 305
But Bloomfields Poems theyre so sweet to hear
They live with me like neighbours all the year
& when the rooks their nests & noises bring
To the tall elm trees at the early spring
So true their rapture with the tale agrees 310
I almost see the Hall between the trees
& when I cross the plank that strides the brook
Oer eastwell green—I even stop to look
For Mary Meldrum & the shooting squire
So green the story comes my thoughts admire 315
Yet cox combs flatterys can have small pretence
To blind the eyes of even common sense
To me tis nonsense—not that I pretend
To teach another how to chuse a friend
Yet truth should guide us all—& proverbs show 320
That truth on falshoods soil can never grow
& when proud people condescend to move
Their silly praise as make-believes for love
Like lanthern in the dark it only shows
They idly judge of people by their cloaths 325

& as our eyes are humble look to find
The same like failings in a persons mind
& having little sense themselves — believe
That such low fools are easy to decieve
I scorn such poor consciet & all its ways 330
& show proud cox combs how I value praise
For he who has such poor contempt of me
To think me foolish can no lover be
For what are lovers but our dearest friends
Truth shows its heart at once & neer pretends 335
We read of servants cast in fortunes way
Who bye & bye grow ladys — so they say
One swallow makes no spring in worlds so wide
All rings are not for weddings till theyre tried
& dreams that hope for luck may end in thrall 340
For truth for one no harvest is for all
Therefore I look on prides soft words as lies
— Praise undeserved is flattery in disguise
& Ive seen flattery walk with dog & gun
& gilded buttons glittering in the sun 345
& wished it further from my milking way
He said "good morn" or tis "a charming day"
& often by my cows would talk & smile
While his bold dogs would lap the milk the while
& scared my cows I could not say "depart" 350
But oft abused the cox comb at my heart
Hed ope his box to offer me a pinch
But I said "nay" & neer gave way an inch
I near was fond of flatterys daubs not I
& never heeded to approach so nigh 355
& he would come close bye my side to walk
But I still shunned the path nor cared to talk
& he would seem anoyed to see me shun
His smiles — & instantly uncocked his gun
Or "tis not loaded Mary" he would say 360
As if twas that which made me steal away
& then more close hed walk down baulk or lane
While I as usual sidled off again

Till he grew weary with my ways at last
& not so much as noticed when he past 365
He'd talk with other girls & said though I
Had got a face that might the proof belie
Yet I was one of lifes low clownish breed
& want of manners made me plain indeed
But foolish fop if I had been so vain 370
As with his gay white stockings to be taen
I then had manners all & every thing
But parsons sanctions & the wedding ring
If his be signs for love theyre none for me
& "old maid Molly" I would sooner be 375

L[ucy]

& none but old maid Mollys past their prime
Would wish for winter in the summer time
& talk of sermons that are out of date
Like an old almanack a year too late
Men thats above your station you despise 380
Their manners you make rudeness in disguise
& smalls the matter if you reason well
They even then the clownish apes excell
Who have no sense to keep their rudeness in
& no more merit then a crooked pin 385
That soon as bent is took & tossed away
& crooked pins are just as good as they
I look upon them as a tiresome weed
& think their rudeness very rude indeed
& yet I laugh at every thing they say 390
But wear deaf ears where rudeness breaks away
& if good fortune should my suit commend
Mind that Id chuse no bumpkin for a friend
No more then nettles should engage my eye
In pleasant gardens when a rose was bye 395

M[ary]

Well you may chuse your garden flowers & take
The rose but chuse it for its sweetness sake

Hope quickly fades beneath a broken pledge
& Ive seen sweeter roses on the hedge
Hedge briars will often make the fingers smart 400
But finer ones will prick you to the heart
— One evening when I went to milk my cows
Some mischief seeking boys with sticks & boughs
Had teazed a whasps nest in the pasture grass
Close to the foot path which I had to pass 405
& as one came & buzzed about my face
I dropt my pails & hurried from the place
Nor dare I venture nigh so chilled with fright
But stopt for Richard till he past at night
When in the mean time who should cross the brig 410
Tapping his boot tops with a switching twig
But Mr Pride — he gave his head a bow
Saying "heigh ho Mary whats the matter now"
& when I told him he proposed a scheme
To stay till night when he would go & team 415
A brimming pail of water on the nest
& drown them all — but I declined the test
Twas just to prove if hed a fool in me
To stay till sun down that he might be free
— Ive read in books that such are nothing nice 420
& look on girls as purchase at a price
— Tis pity that distinctions so confounds
That flimsy paper marked with many pounds
Should make its rude possessors gentlemen
& give them lisence but with tongue & pen 425
To deal out mischief at their idle will
& ruin maids — yet men of honour still
While men with nothing but an honest fame
Who leave the world as poor as when they came
By having nothing bear all sorts of scorn 430
& stand in prides way like a worthless thorn
Worth stands for nought where moneys worth stands first
& poorer folks are sure to be the worst
While wealthy cox combs — O it so provokes
I hate to seet — are always gentle folks 435

— There while I stood as I was forced to stay
Pride sauntered too & would not go away
Holding his snuff box out with sneering smile
Nor offered once to fetch the pail the while
His dogs came round me & I feigned a fear 440
To sidle from him as he chattered near
Poor things it grieved me when he whipt them round
& made them howl & lye upon the ground
Swearing "such freedom he would neer alow
"So Mary stop they will not hurt you now" 445
I felt alarmed — but Richard crossed the lane
& glad I started off to meet the swain
When he came up & twitched me by the gown
& said I hope your lovers not a clown
Indeed he is said I & [Ill] request 450
The mans assistance I esteem the best
When off the cox comb went & tossed his head
& muttered somthing I was vulgar bred
Well never mind if rudeness keeps me free
From such like fops ill manners let it be 455
The girls he ruined witnessed in their shame
His empty praise deserved a worser name
& though the fellow is by fortune fed
Lucks purse is maybe longer then his head
& is pride so preferred with lucks pretence 460
To honest clowns & truth & commonsense

& now the cows are milked & night agen
Leaves free the hovel to the little Wren
The maidens both the simmering brook hath past
Where more stones lie then when they left it last 465
& Marys expectations smiled to see
Her lover waiting neath the maple tree
So loves discourse had end — till eve again
Should call them both to milk upon the plain

Peterborough MS A50, pp.15-16 contains the following passage which was omitted from the final version in Peterborough MS B8, it is not clear whether accidentally or deliberately. It belongs between lines 461 and 462 of the text, and constitutes the final speech by Lucy; we give it here since it provides a resolution to the debate which is otherwise lacking.

Well as a weathercock agen the wind
Your lessons make me of a wavering mind
& somthing in my bosom would be fain
To call poor Simon to its rest again
His plain way never can be loves disguise
To fawn & flatter with new hatching lies
Though his best dress is but a russet brown
& hat that time has robbed of beavers down
His plain hearts like a Gem in meaner case
I cannot put a better in its place

Pastoral 2nd – Jealousy

Loud lowed the happy cows with udders full
To hear the gingling yokes & shrill cum mull
From the two maidens by the hovel side
Who came agen to milk with eventide
The little wren scared at each sudden guest 5
Let drop the feather gathered for his nest
& in the black thorn sat awhile & then
Flew down & pickt the feather up agen
& fluttered round till maidens turned their heads
Then popt into his nest & went to bed 10
The maids resumed their love discourse anew
Half hid by thistles that around them grew
For love is beautys legacy by kind
The grace & harmony of womans mind
For in that soul where no affections spring 15
Beautys vain boast is but a souless thing

Mary

Well Lucy heres the thistle by our side
Shows how weak blossoms may be stung by pride
See how it taunts its head with nought to fear
The very cows seem loath to venture near 20
But heres these daiseys—o so low they spring
They seem to fear the little tiniest thing
Heres one crushed here beneath old Collys tread
The dews seem tears for very anguish shed
So have I thought when tracking mornings dew 25
& Ive smiled too to see it smile anew
& so it is with maids like you & I
Who go beyond themselves & look too high
Theyre sure to stumble ere the journeys oer
Brused like the flower & may be bloom no more 30

[Lucy]

Your hints are easy understood but still
They make a mountain of a little hill

—As to these daiseys crushed by cows—they lie
Mid common things beneath the open skie
While neath this thistle—cut your troubles short 35
Heres many blooms & not a daisy hurt
So turn you[r] idle fancies out of doors
If wealths bad luck—what is it to be poor

Mary

Some have met fortune in a masters house
& in an honest suitor fo[u]nd a spouse 40
Who proud of worth deckt humbleness in silk
To make them mistress of the cows they milk
—& though chance says such chances still may be
For one in favour theres against it three
Some have found golden findings at a fair 45
Some in old ruins met with money there
& some may seek a life time out in vain
Nor find a farthings profit as their gain
So some in blindfold accident may meet
By love & marriage fortune at their feet 50
While others trusting far & hoping all
Instead of rising into ruin fall
—Well call your cows—I feel we yet are friends
If your offended may be truth offends

L[ucy]

Nay mary nay I am not vext a jot 55
But your own foibles have you all forgot
Last may I heard you say—"the vulgar set"
Where none but ploughmen ro[u]nd the garland met
& even yester night did I not see
You scorn the hobnail clowns as well as me 60
Who at their idle praise no notice took
& when they reached your kerchief from the brook
Which the unmannered winds had flirted in
You valued all their kindness not a pin
& when they said "here Mary" turned aside 65
You was not deaf what could it be but pride

& then kind Simon whose good natured ways
Might win a ladys tongue to speak his praise
Did you not scorn him upon may day morn

M[ary]

No Lucy no I did not Simon scorn 70
& as for clowns they are not so by dress
Tis down right ignorance & nothing less
That makes the clown & if I turned away
Twas from their praises which they pleased to pay
Me for the trouble they themselves had taen 75
To thank them Lucy manners were in vain
Had I been free they then had lost their fears
& words had come illsuiting womans ears
Pride some may call it—tis no matter what
You shun low fellows when you notice not 80
For time keeps growing more & more the clown
Wearing to rags like memorys wedding gown
When she & summer married merry may
& la[u]ghed till autumn drove the bride away
For all the praise that wont our tastes to hit 85
Weve lowlived jests fools best mistakes for wit
These in our paths & pastures ever come
& maidens fears must leave their ears at home
A strangers speech gives womans heart alarms
& well meant manners seem intended harms 90
This I alow but follys no disguise
Which any one may know & shut her eyes
But as to Simon you as well might bring
Proofs that I scorn the song I cannot sing
As friend & partner of our evening game 95
Im proud to own him & should feel a shame
To say I scorned one of such gentle ways
Who wins far better folks to speak his praise
The songs he makes I dearly love to hear
& only shun when meddlers interfere 100
How can I help when people make so free
But blush to hear his songs were made on me

—Tis not for me to read mans smiles or sighs
Yet if he loves me tis in this disguise
For never when alone or in a crowd 105
His love escaped him whispered or alowed
For let me tell you I too have my pride
Station can make no gentleman nor hide
True worth from reason—had he spoke in time
This let me say I had not called it crime 110
In one to praise me who so well can praise
Yet he too flatters so my reason says
For in the ballads which the shepherds sing
In pasture huts & by the bubbling spring
His milkmaids show like ladys in such scenes 115
& if he sings of us he makes us queens
His praise of humble life can hardly mean
Yet nought but humble life himself hath seen
& if tis flattery who can think it wrongs
That makes when read or sung such pleasant songs 120
True when that song was sung in which he says
So much of Marys beauty & her praise
I could not think to let him bear the blame
Of praising me—so I denied the name
& if I did could I offend him less 125
I only save his trouble to confess
For if all rumours right & none are wrong
He courts full twenty girls in every song

[Lucy]

Last valentine you know a letter came
Inscribed to Mary—you denied the name 130
& said that many owned that name indeed
& I knew that—you too can write & read
& they who can do neither might know more
Twas meant for them who found it at their door
Yet you already won by clowns—in pride 135
Disda[i]ned to read & cast the thing aside
& when we praised the verses that was read
You blushed with scornful shame & nothing said

& tore it up no doubt as many tear
Their lovers letters when they curl their hair 140

[Mary]

No though the praises cant belong to me
Tis now as near my heart as truth can be
For next my bosom in my hussiff case
(& love has christened that its dearest place)
I keep it — nay believe me look tis here 145
The very same Ill read & you shall hear

Mary thou muse of all my simple themes
Thou fairey sunshine of youths summer dreams
When young love sped upon its happy race
So swift that thought could scarcely keep him pace 150
Again I wooe thee with the voice of ryhme
& idly linger oer that witching time
When in thy sight I felt above the blest
& my soul trembled where that kiss was prest
The very winds that [passed] where thou didst dwell 155
& clouds slow moving oer that happy dell
Where charged with idle messages of sighs
& anxious wishes of my gazing eyes
When e'er thou wandered out at sabbaths hour
My heart grew jealous of each happy flower 160
I thought they crowded in the pleasant ways
To woo thy beauty & to win thy praise
I thought the folding star with eager climb
Gaind evening[s] twilight arch before her time
& moons more soon then they were wont to be 165
Shone out on purpose to be joined by thee
How warmed my hopes oer each imagined smile
Interpreted to omens all the while
As self imagined favours meant for me
Till the heart ached for joy — & all for thee 170
Favours are sweetest joys of lovers toils
Who see their only happiness in smiles
With the[e] earths every trouble vanished bye

& not one cloud soiled loves illumined sky
As when the full moon sheds its proudest ray 175
Night shrinks abashed & startles into day
Thy beauty in my dreams doth joys instill
It ever blest me & it ever will
Serene as glides the gentle brook away
Neath the soft twilight of a summers day 180
Thy timid fondness led to no extreems
But joys as innoscent as infants dreams
I thought thy face so beautiful & shy
That care would never let thee weep or sigh
& still thou dost thy maiden sabbath keep 185
Nor sin hath never gave thee cause to weep
Thou art too fair & beautiful for sin
With angels charms it cannot claim akin
Thou haven of my hopes when ere I see
That lovely face the storm is past with me 190
Thoughts of thy memory glideth in my mind
Forever & no failings eer could find
Thy young rich beauty gilt lifes early hour
Like sudden birth of an unlooked for flower
Nature exulting placed its motto there 195
"This work is mine & where is ought so fair"
Young hope looked on & did in rapture move
& owned the earnest of delight was love
Thy lips were like twin roses which the morn
Kisses & leaves its dewy pearls thereon 200
Yet still as virgin flowers unstained & free
From the bold freedom of the amorous bee
Smiles hung about them as if loath to give
Room to a frown to bid hope cease to live
While thy young bosom at the praise it heard 205
Heaved up & panted like a timid bird
Thy face would win a world to be thy friend
For beautys silence will its suit commend
Thy lovely looks owned raptures sweetest thrill
That words can neither paint or praise but ill 210
O I have gazed with wonder on those eyes

& paid thee angel worship in disguise
& often thought thou wert how beautiful
& felt without thee gayest scenes how dull
& praised thee in my heart ten thousand times 215
In unfeignd fancies & unflattered ryhmes
Yet my heart neer so far forgot its fear
To breath it loudly in thy timid ear
I feared the truth that out of sight did shroud
Would seem but flattery if I spoke it loud 220
& only from the boon such days alow
I had not written what Ive told thee now
So with the sanction of St Valentine
For one day only let me call thee mine
& then like flower pots when their blooms decay 225
To morrow throw the worthless ryhmes away

That is the letter read it if you will
He bids me burn it but I keep it still
Yet dare I say such praise belongs to me
For if I did how foolish should I be 230
& praise so high — but muttered in a crowd
Would make me look more foolish then the proud
& as to beaus can I my self divide
I have not got a heart on either side
In friendships way he stands the first of all 235
But only one as lover I can call
The maid whose beauty many eyes hath won
May out of many sweethearts meet with none

[Lucy]

What not in love wheres reason to deny
Last valentine who saw you read but I 240
The prayer book — aye you blush & well you may
For when I looked you put the book away
I wondered — & nowonder almost stares
When people seem ashamed to read their prayers
So when your back was turned I went to look 245
Beyond excuses — though you shut the book

This mark dropt out compare it with your gown
& where folks marry — leaves was doubled down
Tis all as plain as print beyond a guess
Nor can your best denials make it less 250
For love & marriage if our thoughts incline
Are pleasant prayers to read at valentine
& if young maidens think so wheres the harm
But Simon was the spell that worked the charm

[Mary]

Well now I see you're jealous — & must I 255
To please ones fancies throw all pleasure bye
& when May plays at "crookhorn" saunter near
& bite my thumbs anothers frowns to fear
& hunt the slipper cant I merry be
Without the whisper urged & cast at me 260
The Prayer books self no matter where I read
Could surely stir no fancies in your head
& jokes about such books are far from wise
Truth love & prayer from the same bosom rise
No matter how such things are understood 265
Prayers are not prayers unless our thoughts are good
Nor had you heeded thoughts you fancied mine
Nor filled your head so long with valentine
Had not some other cause below the rest
Lay there consealed — the matter may be guest 270
Tis when I meet old friends in field & town
& laugh & talk that makes another frown
To please all tastes we might ourselves denie
Of daylight & go blind fold neath the sky
Thank day my eyes are good — the springs begun 275
& Ill not shut them for I love the sun
Unless when at the Blindmans bluff we play
At may day eve or when weve got the hay
& ere one blind fold man mistakes the prize
Ill pull myself the kerchief from his eyes 280
So that no maiden may have room to say
She had one cause to frown on such a day

Lucy

Yes Mary certain favours will prevail
Whose cow deserved a mawkin at her tail
But yours when last & yet no shaming thorn 285
Betrayed the Sluggabed that lay till morn
& Simon who pretends his love to me
By doing favours — I can easy see
He was of all the rest the only cause
That broke for you last year the pasture laws 290
You got the garland — twas a shameful sin
That the last comer should a garland win
I almost hated Simon in my spite
Well Lucy well I know that right is right
Said he but who could have the heart to trail 295
A dangling thorn at poor old Collys tail
Though she was last — you was not first — yet friends
Should make a stranger to the place amends
& shes so fair that milks old Colly now
I could not tie a mawkin to her cow 300
— He called you but his friend — pretence to prove
Where friendship went there was not room for love
But yet the shepherd shows more pleasant ways
He made a busk & flowered it for your stays
& begged the old one which your play did break 305
Not for a pattern only — but your sake

Appendix I

Obituary notice of the Countess of Exeter, as copied by Edward Drury from the *Monthly Magazine* III (March 1797), p.239, and sent to Clare (BL MS Egerton 2245, ff.190 and 191). This extract was one of Clare's sources for the story of "Valentine Eve".

From the Monthly Mag. 1797

The amiable woman whose virtues lately gave a lustre to the title of Countess of Exeter, and who died lamented by all who knew her, has something so uncommonly interesting in her history that a detailed sketch of it cannot but be acceptable to every reader of sensibility. When the present Earl was a minor, he married at an early age a lady from whom he was divorced. After the separation his Uncle the late Earl advised him to retire into the country for some time and pass as a private gentleman. Mr. Cecil accordingly bent his course into a remote part of Shropshire, & fixing his residence at an inn in a little rural village, he amused himself there for some months, passing by the name of Jones. As he had plenty of money and was extremely liberal to all about him, some persons in the neighbourhood conceived a notion that he had not come honestly by his riches, grew suspicious of him & shunned his society. They took him for an Indian nabob; and, as he passed along, he often heard the rustics exclaim "There goes the London gentleman." Taking a dislike to his situation at the inn, he sought out a farm house, where he might board & lodge . . . several families had refused to take him in, because he was "too fine a gentleman, and they could not understand how he came by his money." At length he found a situation, which answered his purpose, and, in consideration of his liberal offers, and the knowledge of his possessing money, a farmer fitted him up a room. Here he continued to reside for about two years going up to London twice in the year, and returning with such money as he had occasion for; when he departed the country people thought he went to receive his rents & became more assured of this from his returning with plenty of money. Time hanging heavy on his hands, he purchased some land, on which he intended to build a house, but neither mason nor carpenter would work for him for the reasons mentioned. At length after some grave deliberation & his offering to pay so much money before hand they agreed to finish his work — He did not condescend to contradict the reports spread against him but when the work was done paid every person their demands.

The farmer at whose cottage his Lordship had resided had a daughter, about 17 years of age whose rustic beauties threw at infinite distance, all that his Lordship had ever beheld in the circle of fashion; the softest roses that ever modesty poured upon youth & loveliness, glowed upon her lips...her cheeks were tinged with the divine bloom of Hebe; & the purity of the Huntress Nymph was in her breast:–

"Her lips were red — tho one was thin —
Next to that her chin —
Some bee had stung it newly."

— and whenever any part of her neck or bosom was accidentally displayed the *"Nitor splendens marmore purior"* dazzled the observer's eye.

Although this charming maid was placed in the humble lot of life, his Lordship perceived, that her beauty would adorn, & her virtue shed a lustre on the most elevated situation. One day, when the farmer returned home from his plough, Mr. Cecil frankly told them he liked their daughter, & would marry her, if they would give their consent..."Marry our daughter!" exclaimed the dame, "what to a fine gentleman? No! indeed!" "Yes, marry her, say I," said the husband, "he shall marry her, & she likes him — has he not house and land too & money in plenty to keep her?" In fine the matter was made up and Mr. Cecil married this charming rustic. Masters of every kind were now procured, and, in twelve months' time Mrs. Cecil became an accomplished woman, to the envy of the girls around & to the astonishment of the villagers, who now began to be reconciled to the supposed too fine gentleman.

It was not long before the news arrived of his uncle's death when he found it necessary to repair to town. He accordingly set out, taking his wife with him and on his journey called at the seats of several noblemen, when to the utter astonishment of his wife,. he was welcomed in the most friendly manner. At last they arrived at Burleigh, the beautiful patrimonial seat of his Lordship.

Here they were welcomed with acclamations of joy. As soon as he had settled his affairs, he returned into Shropshire, discovered his rank to his wife's father & mother, put them into the house he had built there & settled 700£ per annum upon them.

He afterwards took his Countess to London, introduced her to the fashionable world, where she was respected, admired, adored, till she died.

Appendix II

John Clare to William Hone

April 1825

Sir

I met tother day with a number of your "Every-day-book" & as I feel a great pleasure in any thing relating to the superstitions & manners of former times I need not say how much entertainment I felt in its perusal   The following miscellaneous superstitions & shadows of customs almost worn out here are at your service to do as you please with — I desire no acknowledgment of them in your numbers as they are worth but ‹little›

On saint Marks Eve it is still a custom about us for young maids who are some times joind by young men to make the "dumb cake" a mystical ceremony which has lost its origin & in some countys may have ceasd altogether — the number of the partys is never to exceed three   they meet in silence & at twelve oclock they eat it still silent for if one speaks the spell is broken   when they have done they walk up to bed backwards & those that are to be married see the likness of their sweet hearts hurrying after them as if they wanted to catch them before they get to bed but the maids being apprised of this before hand take care nearly to undress them selves before they start & are ready to slip into bed before they are caught & if nothing is seen the token is sure to be heard in a knocking at the doors or rustling in the house as soon as they have left & to be convinced that it comes from nothing else but the desired cause they take care to turn out the cats & dogs on that night in particular   those that are to dye unwed see nor hear nothing but have terrible dreams which are sure to be of graves & rings that fit no finger & if they do crumble into dust as soon as on — there is another dumb ceremony of eating the yolk of an egg in silence & filling the shell with salt when the sweetheart is sure to make his appearance in some way or other before morning   on this same night too the more stout hearted watch the church Poach   they go in the evening & lay a branch of any tree or flower in the Poach & then return home & wait till 12 o clock at night when two goes as far as the church gate & one stays till the other fetches the bough   if they are to be married they will see their own persons hanging on the arms of their future husbands with the priest &c as if going to be married & as many couples of bride men & maidens as they shall see following them so many months shall it be ere they are married & if they are to dye unwed then the procession that passes them is a funeral a coffin coverd with a white sheet appears to be born by shadows without heads & the number of carriers betokens the number of years that the partys are to live — this as terrible as it seems is a custom very often practiced — & an odd character who had no fear calld Ben Barr a prophet usd to watch the poach every year & pretended to know the fates of every one in the villages round as who should be married or dye in the year but as a few pence generally predicted a good omen he seldom prophecied the deaths of his believers

On Whit sunday the youth of both sexes used to meet at a Fountain calld "East well" to drink spring water as [a] charm for good luck & a preventative of disease this was undoubtly a roman catholic custom as some of the troughs remain still that betoken [it] to have been an holy well the initials of names & crosses rudely cut with knives are still visible — a pond a league distant from this spring is still famous for cureing many diseases & people go often on spring mornings to drink it tho the custom of meeting at the spring on Whitsunday to drink sugar & water has been abolished ever since the inclosure

On Holy thursday they go round the fields opening the meres or land marks were they still keep up an ancient custom of scrambling in the mere holes for sugar plumbs & running races for cross shittles in which old & young often join — there is also a curious superstition which has forgotten the cause in which it origionated — young boys & girls the sons & daughters go on purpose to be placed on their heads in the mere or *

On may day a multiplicity of sports & customs are still observed but some of them are so popular that they need no mention yet they differ in places — about us the first cow that is turnd upon the pasture gets the Garland & the last has the mawkin a large

* The cross presumably refers to a continuation of this passage which has not so far been traced. The use of such signs is common practice in Clare MSS – Eds.

branch of thorns tyd to her tail the young men who wish to win the favour of their favourites wait on the green till a late hour & then drive out the cows of the maiden whom they love who of course wins the garland & in the evening she is considerd the Queen of the May & the man wether her favourite or not claims her as his partner for the dance at night a custom that she dare not refuse to comply with as she woud loose her reputation & sweet heart into the bargain & grow into a byeword for a shrew & be shund accordingly

On Holy rood day it is faithfully & confidentily believd both by old & young that the Devil goes a nutting on that day & I have heard a many people affirm that they once thought it a tale till they ventured to the woods on that day when they smelt such a strong smell of birmstone as nearly stifled them before they coud escape out again — & the cow boy to his great dissapointment finds that the devil will not even let his black berrys alone & he believes them after that day to be poisend by his touch

On St Tomases Eve it is a common custom for the young girls to lay a red peeld onion under their pillows to dream of their sweet hearts — Loves annals are overrunning with these superstitions yet there is one on New Years Eve that I think you woud not have passd over in silence had you known of it On the first moon in the new year young men & maids look through a silk hankerchief (that has been drawn through a ring) at the New moon & as many moons as each person sees through it as many years will they be ere they are married

The Morris Dance is very popular now with us they begin to go round the week before christmass — it appears to have been a burlesque parody on some popular story at the time but it has been so mutilated by its different performers that I coud not make sense of it tho I tryd to transcribe from the mouths of 3 or four persons who had all been actors in it there are 4 characters 2 of them the Kean & Young of the piece are finely dressd their hats are deckorated with carpenters dale shavings & cut paper & without side their cloaths they wear a white shirt hung with ribbons of different colors a silk hankerchief serves them for a sash & another slung over their shoulders is a belt for their swords which are some times real & sometimes wooden ones the third character is a sort of Buffoon grotesquely dressd with a hunch back & a ball hung between his legs together with a tail trailing behind him his face is blacked & he generaly carrys in his hand a hugh club the 4th is a docter dressd as much in character as their taste or circumstances allows – the plot of the thing is some thing as follows – the Kean of the Drama steps in first & on speaking a sort of prologue discovers him self to be a no less personage then the king of Egypt his errand appears to be to demand his lost son who seems to have married a lady not worthy the heir of Egypt or to be confined in prison for it is so destitute of common sense that you can not tell which & [as] they refuse his enquireys his champion prince George is calld in who after talking a great deal of his wonderful feats in slaying dragons & hacking his enemeys as small as flyes begins a dialogue with his majesty then the fool is introduced with his bell who gives a humerous description of himself & his abilitys when all three joins in the dialogue & instantly a quarrel is created between the Kean & Young from what cause I know not & they draw their swords & fight the fool gets between them to part them & pretending to be wounded by the king falls down as dead when the other confesses that the murderd man is the kings own son in disguise whose rage is instantly turnd to sorrow & the docter is calld in & a large reward is offerd him if he can restore him to life who after enumerating his vast powers in medical skill & knowledge declares the person to be only in a trance & on the docters touching him he rises & they all join hands & end the Drama with a dance & Song —

There used to be a common custom — when old men & women & childern used to go stone gathering in the fields if one found a stone with a hole in it to put a string thro it & hang it at the masters coat button behind where if he did not discover it in a certain time they fell laughing & calling out "riddy riddy wry rump" & claimed the boon of a largess when the stone gathering was finished — from what scourse could such a strange custom origionate — inclosure came & destroyed it with hundreds of others — leaving in its place nothing but a love for doing neighbours a mischief & public house oratory that dwells upon mob law as absolute justice

I am sorry to bring a dirty reality so near your poetical description of plough monday but I think a custom of half the northern countys will not be unwelcome on this day in our county (Northamptonshire) & in the neighbouring ones of Rutland Lincoln Cambridge &c it is the custom for the plough boys (whose anxiety for the sport almost wakens before the morning) to meet at the black smiths shop to dress themselves & get ready not with white shirts & ribons but to black their faces with a mixture of soot & grease & all that will not under go this are reckond unworthy of the sport & excluded the company — they get an old skeleton of a plough with out share or colter & attach to it a waggon rope in which sticks are loopd & on each side these sticks the boys take their station they are calld plough bullocks the stoutest among them is selected for the holder of the plough & thus equipd they pull it round the village from door to door for what they can get when they have gotten beer at the door they run the "wind up" as they call it to please their benefactors & chusing the dirtiest place in the yard he that gets the most mauled & complains of it the least is reckoned a brave fellow in this wind up they try to entangle the holder of the plough in the ropes who by superior strength not only keeps from tumbling but contrives by dextorusly manoeuring & throwing the plough to get most of the plough bullocks wound up in their own ‹traces› — to those that will not give to them they let loose their mischief by pulling up shoe scrapers at the door or gate posts & winding up the person in the rope & as it is reckoned a lawless day the constable will rarely interefere if calld upon — several of the boys of the neighbouring villages used to meet at Milton Hall to get beer were they had it without stint when before the wind up commenced the different villagers usd to hang each others ploughs together & pull against them to try which was the strongest — which caused such confusion of quarreling that it was abolished — the men grown servants 3 or 4 of them go round the Village dressd up in a grotesque manner they are calld the "plough witches" 2 of them has their faces blackd & a hunch back of straw stuffd into their smock frocks their hats are tyd up into a three cockd form & figured with chalk in their hands they carry a beesom & a spoon filld with soot & grease to sweep the dirt on & black the faces of the servants maids they happen to meet with who generally take care to keep out of the way the "she witch" as he is calld is dressd up in a laughable joanish manner in womans cloaths he has no hunch back & his face is ruddled they carry a box with half pence in it which they shake as the come to the door — at night the bullocks & witches meet together in a sociable party & enjoy their supper cake & ale — this is the real custom of plough monday which "is known to this day"

Appendix III

From a letter from Clare to J.A. Hessey, after 13 October 1823 (Peterborough MS A46, pp.91-4); the first part of the letter is in Letters, *pp.286-7. Gaps and tears in the MS have been supplied in square brackets; conjectures are marked with a question mark.*

. . . I shall go on to fill up this sheet with remarks upon the different fashions of poetry that I have had the chance of meeting with — in Chausers time that illustrious father of an increasing family the simplest dress of the muses natures home spun linsey wolsey seems to have been reckon[ed] the best & there is no proofs to the contra[r]y against it for it has wor[n] out the language or nearly & is nature still as fresh as ever [Ere ?] Spencer that beautiful romance of the muses appeard the restless[ness] after knighthood was in fashion & near a poem was sanctioned by the public unless it had a knight of some sort or other for its hero & knights were plenty to serve them dazzling in all the hues of the rain bow red blue green & every other color then fashion sickened & pastorals was the vogue the knights in shining armour & the wailing ladys in haunted towers were left to get on as they coud for the simpler company of Shepherds piping to their Sheep & Shepherdesses under the shades of awthorns by murmuring fountains this at length grew wearisome & they forsook them grasshopping about brook sides & smooth meadows with damons & Phillises to sing of beds of down & nymphs without peticoats & naked breasts "Courting the hand & suing to be prest["] & ravishing kisses & smutty prophecys of ogling eyes till on the puritan side of the question the muses were looked on as a set of whores of Babylon it might be exaggerated but they had got bad enough no doubt well fashion ceasd its [   ] and turned the stream but themes on high life woud not ease the [polution ?] [flattery ?] coud not wash out the stains virtue had fled & found shelter [am]ong the poor simple discard[ed sh]epherds & sheperdesses & they took it in their heads to follow her once more a pastoralizing but not in the true nature & simplicity of the bards of Elizabeth that glorious era of poesy that golden age of Englands muses no they coud not go so far they coud not stoop so low it was vulgar so they fashiond an "arcadia" for themselves were the Right honorable Lords Damons Strephons &c (for they were more like lords then shepherds) sprucd it about in every picture with crooks in their hands bowing to my ladys Delias Chloes Phillises &c & presenting a garland of flowers or like the song "a bunsh of blue ribbons to tye up my hair" while the ladys were busy binding the horns of their rams with festoons of vine leaves or ivy sometimes they discorsed learnedly about Virgils beach tree & the goats of Theocritus admiring the classic purity of the one & the rustic simplicity [of the other] finse shepherds these to track the fallow clods & stand the heats of summer nor woud the face of nature do as they found it it was too simple [ ] the gentl[e]-men poets was too fastidious to be pleasd with the brook rippling its shells & pebbles instead of these it purld over golden sands pearls & chrystal — instead of the wild flowers of the wilderness growing [on] its brink it was dizend out with daffodills narsissus lilys &c &c [in] lieu of the leaning willows picturing their pale shadows in the stream we had the jesamine & the myrtle these were bowers very suitable for the lady shepherdesses acting in these gingerbread dreamas these simpering sweet meats who sat keeping their flocks in silks & satins while their wooers in the dresses of courtiers sat piping to please them upon pipes made of ivory with crooks of silver & the shafts studded with rubies & what did all this tinsel amount too a bombastical nothing[1] I had the hardihood once to ask a friend wethers these ornaments were ever natives of english senery & wether canarys & humming birds as suitable appendages were never known to live wild in this country & my credulity was laughd at as it deser[v]d for I verrily fancyd they might but enough of these glittering bastard pastorals which are no more like what they woud pretend to be then a jewellers shop or the mimic splendor of pallaces is to the mild dreamy [*blank*]& sublime mysterys of heaven — time grew sick of em or at least fashion did & elbowd shepherds with their

[1] It was too vulgar to call things by their own names — so that the dead nettle had the good fortune to get nighted with the fine title of "Archangel" by some poet of this "golden age" & the nettle ought to be thankful for his lordships pastoral condesencion such things may be thought wearisome trifles to mention but it is mentioned to illustrate a trifling subject

silver crook & shepherdesses with their rubies all out of the consern to gether poetry now took a new turn it must have somone sanctiond by time for its hero or at any rate be cram full of learned allusions & digressions about the ancients their manners customs or somthing   the sun coud not rise in the poets verses without his beams being likend to the golden hair of Apollo   brooks coud not flow in them without a tagd digression [   ] Horaces blandusian fountain — the simpering misses & maudlin mistresses of poets were to be delighted & won by fine names &c was she fair then she was like Venus & the lover of course might readily hope the compliment returnd in fancying him her adonis   had she roses on her cheeks wether her own or not was no signification were they did not stand about trifles thean she was Hebe was she tall then Diana the huntress was aluded too & if her compexion wore none of these classic beautys there were names enough in read[i]ness to suit even if she was a gipsey or more politly a "dark beauty"   Sappho might be taken at a venture or luna as the queen of swathy night even "lines on ladys lapdogs["] caught the distemper & cato & pompey & Brutus & Cesar was deemd nessesary to embelish such trifles[2]   for the madness we no doubt are indebted to the colledge poets who might love t[o] show their reading   however this is in part done away tho not witho[ut] other editions for this prolific age d[ea]ls in all sorts of out[landish ?] comoditys in gods goddesses sh[epherds] shepherdesses goths vandals & monsters of all sorts & [si]zes f[oreig]n witches of atlas the black & brown dwarf[s of] scots [sup]erstition but past[orals] the true pastorals seem to b[e left] badly off yet for Bloomf[ield] our "english theocritus" is laid bye & Wordsworth they [affect ?] to despise popes tinsel pastorals are yet admird & in a[n essay] written in the guardian by himself in [prais]e of himself he [says they] are "somthing better" then pastorals   [to] be sure poor simple nature cannot claim them & the fash[ionable] reader can   he is now backd by an high authority [who not con]tent with placing him on the highest pinacle of fame woud sac[rifice t]he fame of another to make room for his

[2] "The eyes rained showers" aye "seas of tears" where shed over moultering parrots & dying lapdogs

favourite by saying that pope was a poet & that Cowper was none by the bye high [author]itys will act as silly as little ones sometimes well be it so but give [me the] "task" & take all the popes that ever reignd in rome o[r in ?] arcadia & I am content[3] a few of our living poets are lauded & f[awn ?]ed over with praises as equal & by some superior to Spencer & Shakespear & Milton but wh[en ?] opinions & Critisisms are blanks when the dust of 3 centurys [lies ?] upon their fine gilt covers & white paper I fear time will have d[one] somthing towards spoiling the picture making the highest grow dim a gre[at] distance from the mighty & the rest forgotten nothings — it is said that 2 of the [same] trade cannot agree I would not be thought to urge malice or envy in this [ ] for when the great structures fall the little cottage must follow which leav[es] chance without a remedy its only a surmise a sort of self dread time wil[l] us when we are no longer worthy of notice & how can we help it — the mo[st of ?] common praise takes the course of the stream the sea has its flow & [ ] fasion is the end of one & nature the other but the gradual eleva[tion of] a public name that steals as it were on the praises of the few still [grows ?] in strength unpercievd by the many climbing step by step up that env[ious] eminence of futuritys esteem which like Jacobs ladder dream seems [reaching ?] at eternity this in my opinon is the bes[t]ng shadow of [fame ?]

yours &c &c [J] Clare

Rough sketch of an Essay sent to the London Mag: & never noticd

3 tis the fashion now to talk about Pope & his poetry merely for the sake of talking & Mr Roscoe favours the reading public with his "last letter to Bowles" & Bowles with his "final appeal to the Public" about 3 times a year & Mr Bowles by the bye is as ready with dealing out lyes (or as fashion miscalls the[m] opin[i]ions & retracting them as pliantly as his old acquaintance the "Vicar of Bray"

ach *v.* ache
addle *v.* earn
agen *adv.* again
agen *prep.* against
amain *adv.* at once
ance *n.* ? aniseed
An old droll woman Granny Bains, the old woman from whom Clare learnt many songs and stories
apple scope *n.* apple scoop, often made from the shank bones of sheep. 'Their primary purpose was to scoop the pulp from inside one apple, leaving the skin empty and crumpled, for the benefit of toothless old people who still wanted to eat raw apple, or possibly for infants' (Jean Wellanby, *Odd Objects*, St Ives, Cambs.: Norris Library, 1983, pp.7-9). Used by *Australopitheas prometheus* several hundred thousand years ago.
ast as it

bands *n.pl.* banns
ba(u)lk *n.* strip of grass between ploughed fields
beaver *n.* hat, originally of beaver fur
beavering hour *n.* time for a break for refreshment
beesom *n.* broom of twigs
beguy *inter.* a common word of interjection
bindweed *n.* *Convolvulus arvensis*
birmstone *n.* brimstone
black thorn *n.* sloe, *Prunus spinosa*
blast *n.* exciting time, merry-making
bleb *v.* to cover with drops, blob
blindmens b(l)uff *n.* a children's game in which a person with a blindfold tries to catch others
blobbd *v.* blabbed
Bloomfields Poems there are eight volumes of Bloomfield dated 1819-1824 in Clare's library at Northampton
bluecap *n.* blue tit, *Parus caeruleus*
boarden *adj.* boarded, made of boards

boon *n.* gift of food and drink
bout *adv.* about
bran spanking *adj.* brand new, smart
breath *v.* breathe
brig *n.* bridge
broach *n.* brooch
broken crutch 'The Broken Crutch, a Tale', pp.51-74 of Bloomfield's *Wild Flowers* (1819)
bunting *n.* chaffinch, *Fringilla coelebs,* also known as pink, spink, or hedge-sparrow
burr *n.* haziness or mist, covering or encircling the moon
busk *n.* bodice or sometimes a stiffener for a bodice
butchers cleaver *n.* the Pleiades, see J.B. Smith: 'John Clare's Constellations', *John Clare Society Journal,* IX (July 1990), for this and other astronomical references in the present glossary
by *v.* buy, perhaps Clare's attempt to reproduce the Jew's voice
by times *adv.* betimes

cade, cady *adj.* reared by hand, tame, pet
The candle curld winding sheets The candle-smoke rose in spirals, a sign of imminent death
card *v.* cared cast their opinions, weighed their opinions
chelp *v.* chirp
childer(n) *n.pl.* children
choak *v.* choke
cloaths *n.pl.* clothes
clock *v.* clip-clop
close *n.* enclosed field, usually for pasturing cattle
clot hopper *n.* clodhopper, yokel, stupid fellow
clown *n.* rustic, yokel, labourer
clumb *past tense* climbed
Colly *n.* cottager's cow, black appearing to be the primitive meaning of colly: its original application was probably to a black cow
consiet *v.* think
cot(t) *n.* cottage
courtsey *n.* curtsey

covert   cover it
coy *v.*   coax, entice
crab *n.*   crab-apple, *Malus sylvestris*
crack *v.*   boast
crane *n.*   as in 'act the crane': 'A man holds in his hand a long stick with another tied at the top in the form of an L reversed, which represents the long neck and beak of the crane. This, with himself, is entirely covered with a large sheet. He mostly makes excellent sport, as he puts the whole company to the rout, picking out the young girls, and pecking at the bald heads of the old men...' (Clare's description in the Introduction to *The Village Minstrel*, 1821)
crimp *v.*   ripple, ruffle, wrinkle
crinkd *adj.*   crinkled
crivisd *adj.*   creviced
Cromwells castle   Woodcroft Castle near Helpston. See *The Village Minstrel*, lines 951-1038 for Clare's account of the desperate encounter between Michael Hudson, the king's chaplain, and Cromwell's men (*Early Poems*, II, pp.163-7). The story is told in Walter Scott's *Woodstock*. In Clare's day the castle was the home of his friends, the Bellairs family
crookhorn *n.*   a game
cross plumb shittles *n.*   a game played by knocking down skittles with a weighted string hanging from a cross
cross row *n.*   Christ-cross-row, the alphabet, therefore 'as plain as the alphabet'
cuckoo songs *n.pl.*   may refer to the custom on 15 October, St Luke's Day, of making fun of contented cuckolds; see William Hone, *The Every-Day Book*, vol. 1 (1826), pp.1386-8
cum mull *n.*   common call for cows to come for milking
curdled *v.*   rippled
curry combs *n.pl.*   combs or instruments of metal used for currying horses etc.

dale *n.*   deal
damsin *n.*   damson
dash *n.*   part of the old-fashioned upright churn called the 'dash'

churn and not to be used of the barrelchurn which has a revolving dash

dead *n.* death

dicks night waggon *n.* the seven bright stars of the Plough

dissabille *n.* (from *en déshabille*) incomplete state of dress

dizen *v.* dress showily, adorn

dot do it

duck & drake *n.* a game of skimming flat pieces of stone across the surface of still water

duck neath water *n.* a game in which the players run, two by two, in rapid succession under a handkerchief held up by two others

dumb cake *n.* a cake made in silence on St Mark's Eve, with numerous ceremonies, by maids, to discover their future husbands. For a description of this custom see Clare's letter to William Hone, Appendix II

dursn't *v.* dared not

Eastwells fountain side *n.* In his Autobiography, Clare writes about going to 'Eastwell on a Sunday to drink sugar and water at the springhead but enclosure came'

eastwell green *n.* just south of the railway line at Helpston, now the site occupied by Arborfield Paper Mill

eke *v.* increase

eldern *n.* elder tree, *Sambucus nigra*

em sens *prn.* themselves

eve *n.* eave

fa(i)ring *n.* present bought at a fair

feign *v.* fain

fent *adj.* faint

fis'es *n.* fists

fissles *n.* thistles

fold *v.* place sheep in the fold

folding star *n.* a star rising at folding-time, an evening star

fort for it

freak *n.* notion, fancy, trick, jest

friends *n.pl.* the eighteenth-century use includes relations

fussy *adj.* fondling

gabbering (man) *adj.* one who has the gift of the gab, hence a salesman, a pedlar
gait a water *n.* two buckets carried with a yoke
garland *n.* May garland won by the milkmaid who is earliest afield on May day
gauled *adj.* rubbed sore
gen *adv.* again
gen *prep.* against
giles *n.* typical name for a farm servant
gingle *v.* jingle
gogd *v.* jogged
Goody *n.* an old woman, widow
goss *n.* gorse, furze, *Ulex europaeus*
grain *n.* large branch of a tree, bough
guisd *adj.* disguised
gun *v.* began

haloo *v., inter.* hallo
harp *v.* dwell on, keep repeating
heft *n.* haft, handle
hirple *v.* stumble, walk lame, limp
his fears might consiet his fears might be making him imagine things
hobbies *n.pl.* hobby-horses, overdressed yokels
Hodge *n.* typical name for an agricultural labourer
hoes *n.* hose (worsted)
hollow *v.* holler, hollo
Holy rood day 14 September in the church calendar. Nutting was customary on this day
hounds & hunters *n.* a game in which one person is given a start and lays a trail followed by the others
housleek *n.* *Sempervivum tectorum*, carefully cultivated on the thatch of cottages as a charm against lightning (see G. Grigson, *The Englishman's Flora*, 1955, p.183)
hovel *n.* animal shed in a field
hugh *adj.* huge
hunt the slipper *n.* an indoor game in which the players sit in

a ring and pass covertly a slipper from one to another with a remaining player standing in the middle and trying to get hold of it

hurded *adj.* hoarded

hussif case *n.* small case to contain sewing materials

ingenious *adj.* ingenuous, ignorant

jelt *v.* throw, fling

joanish *adj.* like a stereotypical rustic female: 'joan' is a generic name for a rustic female

joseph in the bible see Genesis 40 and 41

Kean and Young, Edmund Kean (1787-1833) and Charles Young (1777-1856) actors. See *DNB*

king cup *n.* marsh marigold, *Caltha palustris*

knap *v.* snap with the teeth, bite, nibble

kitling *n.* kitten

knitting sheath, nitting skeath *n.* see Jean Mellanby, *Odd Objects* (St Ives, Cambs.: Norris Library, 1983), pp.62-5, with illustrations and full description of use. There is a collection at the Dales Folk Museum, Hawes, N. Yorks. 'A typical sheath is a straight stick of about eight inches long. One end is tapered to fit into the knitter's belt or waistband. The other is pierced to a depth of about two inches, so that the right hand needle can be pushed into it... The stick or sheath was tucked into the right side of the waistbelt and its purpose was to hold one needle firm and so free the fingers of the right hand. When the needles were curved, as they used to be, the knitter held the work very close to the tips of the fingers, and so could achieve knitting speeds quite beyond us today. To some extent the weight of the work could be taken by the rigid needle, but there were other devices for this, such as pins and hooks to hold it on to the dress. There were also hooks for the ball of wool, and a few knitters used a *broach*, a wooden peg inside the bale of wool which could be tucked into the clog or shoe. With this equipment the knitter could keep going while walking.'

lambtoe *n.* the common bird's-foot trefoil, *Lotus corniculatus*

Lammas *n.* 1 August, 'Loaf Mass' or 'Bread Mass', a feast of thanksgiving for the first fruits of corn (see William Hone, *The Every-Day Book*, vol. I, 1826, p.1063)

land rail *n.* corncrake, *Crex crex*

lanthern *n.* lantern

lap *v.* wrap, fold

lare *n.* lair, rest, bed

learn *v.* often used for teach

lieve *v.* believe

linnet *n.* Clare refers to the red headed linnet, *Acanthus flammea*, the green linnet, *Carduelis chloris*, the brown linnet or furze linnet, *Acanthus cannabina*

loan *adj.* lone

loath *adj.* loth

loose *v.* lose

lost love letter *n.* a game probably resembling Postman's Knock

love knott platts *n.pl.* spells or charms, made by rustics, from the blades of the oat, or wheat, and sometimes from the reed blade

lown *n.* loon, scamp, peasant

lunging *v.* wandering

martinmass *n.* St Martin's Day, 11 November

Mary Meldrum & the shooting squire Robert Bloomfield's 'The Broken Crutch, a Tale', pp.51-74 of *Wild Flowers* (1819)

mavis *n.* mistle thrush or storm cock, *Turdus viscivorus*

mawkin *n.* a) a stuffed figure of shreds and patches, scarecrow, b) a bunch of nettles and thistles tied to the tail of the last cow on the pasture on May day and therefore a disgrace to the milkmaid

may balls *n.pl.* a game of throwing balls made of flowers over a rope hung in the street

mayday statute *n.* May day fair

Maze *n.* a game, probably nine peg morris

mighis *n.* midges

midsummer cushion *n.* 'It is a very old custom among villagers in summer time to stick a piece of greensward full of field flowers & place it as an ornament in their cottages which ornaments are called Midsummer Cushions' (Clare)

Milton Hall   the ancestral home of the Fitzwilliams, at Peterborough

mole *n.*   there are numerous superstitions concerning moles on the human body

morn past opinions   the morning was spent in the exchange of opinions

mort *n.*   lot, large number

near *adv.*   ne'er

neer *adv.*   nearly, when not meaning 'ne'er'

netterd *n.*   neat herd, herd-boy

niggard *adj.*   of poor quality

nigh as fourpence a groat is   as near as fourpence is to the value of a groat, i.e., equal in value

nine peg morris *n.*   squares were cut in the turf and stones or pegs were placed alternately by the players to prevent an adversary from laying three in a row

nitting skeath   see knitting sheath

nock up *v.*   arouse by knocking at a door

nook *n.*   angular corner of a field

nott *n.*   knot

nudge *v.*   hint at, draw attention to

Oakley hall *n.*   Clare probably has Woodcroft Castle in mind, see Cromwells castle

pad *n.*   path

pails *n.*   palings

pall *n.*   cloth that covers the coffin

pash *v.*   bruise, beat into small pieces

passing an odd crow   Clare frequently comments on the superstition that to see a single crow is bad luck

passing bell *n.*   bell tolled at a funeral

perk *adj.*   pert

pharoahs baker   see Genesis 40: 16-22

pinch back *n.*   pinchbeck, goldlike alloy of copper used in cheap jewellery, counterfeit, sham

pismire *n.* ant, *Leontodon taraxcum*
plash *n.* splash
plashing *adj.* splashing
plough witch monday the first Monday after Twelfthday, originally the day on which the husbandmen resumed their labours after the Christmas festivities. Derived from the ancient Feast of Fools
pluft *adj.* swollen, bloated, puffy
plumb *n.* plum
poach *n.* porch
poesy *n.* posy
prayer book (read the) i.e. look over the marriage-service
presevere *v.* persevere
presisted *v.* persisted
prog *v.* prod, poke
prund *v.* pruned, preened
pudgy *adj.* puddly, muddy
puer *adj.* pure

quere *adj.* queer

'racula *n.* auricula
rallied down *v.* shot down
ramp *v.* romp
reciept *n.* recipe
red cap *n.* goldfinch, *Carduelis carduelis*
road to troy *n.* a game, probably nine peg morris
rout *n.* route
ruddle *n.* red stain (made from earth) used to mark sheep
rund *v.* ran
runnel *n.* stream, brook, rill
rushing (fair) *adj.* noisy, bustling

saint marks eve 24 April, the occasion for watching the church for unquiet spirits (see William Hone, *The Every-Day Book*, Vol. II, 1827, p.548)
St Thomas' eve 21 December. A day for 'gooding' i.e. for widows to collect gifts
Sawney *adj.* idle

scape *v.* escape
scrambd *v.* scrambled
scratting *v.* scratching
seet see it
Sensitive *n.* any of several plants of the genus Mimosa with leaves sensitive to tactile stimulation
seven stars *n.pl.* the Pleiades
shagger-down *adj.* layabout
shanny *adj.* shy, shamefaced
shepherds lamp *n.* the first star that rises after sun-set, the evening star, Jupiter
shill *adj.* shrill
shool *v.* stroll, saunter lazily
shooting north lights *n.pl.* Aurora borealis or northern lights
shoyness *n.* shyness
sideling *adj.* sidelong
sidle *v.* saunter, meander
sile *v.* faint, sink, subside gradually
sin *conj.* since
skait *v.* skate
skew *v.* shy, look askance
slaum *v.* slobber, blubber, smear
slive *v.* slove (past tense), slide, slip, sneak, skulk
sluggabed *n.* one who lies abed too long in the morning
sluthering *adj.* slithering
snufted *v.* snuffed
som'at *n.* something
soodle *v.* linger, dawdle, saunter
spirey *adj.* pointing and tapering like a spire
stard *v.* stared
stays *n.pl.* stiffener for bodice
stranger *adj.* belonging to a stranger
strimes *v.* measures
sturt *v.* start, disturb
style *n.* stile
surley *adv.* surely
swee *v.* swing, sway
sweet wort *n.* a sweet-flavoured wort, any plant of a sweet taste

swop *v.* swoop, pounce

taen *pp.* taken
take yer trundle get on with it your own way
taw *n.* marble
taylors yardband *n.* the belt of Orion
tazzeld *adj.* entangled
team *v.* pour out, empty
tear / Their lovers letters when they curl their hair i.e. make curling papers out of scraps of letters
teazle *n.* teasel, *Dipsacus fullonum*
tended *v.* intended
then *conj.* than
third ague *n.* tertian ague
threble *adj.* treble
tokening *v.* betokening
Topal Fair Torpel in the parish of Ufford. Torpel Manor was the seat of one of the Norman barons of Peterborough Abbey and remains of his castle still survive
tother *pron.* the other
touchmenot *n.* name for two different kinds of plants with seed-vessels which burst at a touch, a) squirting cucumber; b) yellow balsam, *Impatiens Nolitangere*, the ripe capsules of which split open with a jerk on being touched
town *n.* village
trig *adj.* neat
trapping *v.* behaving treacherously
tung *v.* struck

veigle *v.* inveigle, enquire cunningly

were *adv.* where
weigling *v.* inveigling
wet *v.* whet
wet rest *n.* rest as a result of the rain
wew *n., v.* call like an owl, pewit etc.
window shuts *n.* shutters
witching *adj.* bewitching

woodbine *n.* honeysuckle, *Lonicera periclymenun*
wort *n.* see sweet wort
wowl *v.* howl, shriek

youngling *adj.* youthful
your you are